Somebody's Knock-In At Your Door

Somebody's Knock-in At Your Door

A Personal Reflection on
The Call to Christian Vocation, Ministry, and Service

Rev. Frederick Douglas, Jr., Ph.D.

FOREWORD BY: Reverend Dr. Zan W. Holmes, Jr.

Orman Press

Somebody's Knock-in At Your Door

A Personal Reflection on

The Call to Christian Vocation,

Ministry, and Service

Frederick Douglas, Jr., Ph.D.

Orman Press, Inc.
Lithonia, GA

ISBN: 1-891773-82-8

Printed In the United States of America

10 9 8 7 6 5 4 3 2 1

Dedication

This book is dedicated to the loving memory of my grandmothers, Carrie and Mary; the former nourished and supervised me during my early church life; the latter taught me to recite scripture, and on her death-bed, clutched my hands and prayed that God would give me a "new job". Also, this book is dedicated to Valerie, my wife, who like no other human being has consistently walked the Christian journey with me since the moment I first believed and responded to God's call, and to Steven and Tezrin, my children, who inspire me to be a worthy role model, along with my parents, Frederick, Sr., and Arlena who taught me to love God, my neighbor and myself.

Contents

Foreword

Christendom generally endorses the call to individuals, specific groups, congregations and the Church. Followers avow that call is the medium the Godhead selects to disclose intended roles as disciples. In **Somebody's Knock-in at Your Door**, Reverend Frederick Douglas, Jr. proposes the call should be an active, reciprocal communication between the Godhead and the summoned children of God. He conveys that the call is a fellowship which should be entered in good faith. Therefore, it is necessary to commit to canceling firmly held personal agendas. Such a commitment unites the children of God to this sacred covenant.

From the writings of consensus ancient theologians, the Church has inherited a treasured corpus of systematic thought about the call. Contemporary scholarship publishes hermeneutical viewpoints about this divine invitation. Across denominations, well-organized reference resources guide candidates in their quest for ordained ministry, careers in Christian vocation, and service in a host of mission fields.

This book shows evidence of much reliance on these valuable literary resources. However, Reverend Douglas draws our attention to a uniquely different stream. His perspective about the call is influenced by intimate personal reflection. Recollection of authentic call stories and empirical evidence of the call acting in people he knows has motivated him to record these perspectives. Specific names and details are omitted; only the author's insights and interpretations enter the conversation.

Fondly remembered, but again, not revealed, are the candidates the author counseled, mentored, and/or formally examined during a six year tenure serving the Conference Board of Ordained Ministry. Then, there were the five parishioners who emerged from the pew to the pulpit. God placed them under Reverend Douglas' watch-care during his second appointment to the local church.

The book before you is a collection of related narratives. It paints a lived portrait of the call which blends scripture, story, theology and appropriate documentation. A clear use of metaphor encourages critical thinking. Though not an autobiographical sketch, Somebody's Knock-in at Your Door, shares a few of the writer's call testimonies. Ironically, some of my private call experience resonated with his. Of central concern for Reverend Douglas is that the reader explores untapped call nuances with deeper introspection.

Throughout, Reverend Douglas exhibits the heart of a pastor. His work affirms his personal relationship with God. He conveys that we are not isolated with the joys, concerns and struggles associated with accepting the call. Foremost, he leaves readers with fresh common ground to dialogue about the call.

Whether you are currently carrying out your call; need clarity as you follow Jesus Christ; contemplated, denied or are oblivious to the call; are churched, unchurched or profess no belief, this book is for you.

Reverend Dr. Zan W. Holmes, Jr.

ACKNOWLEDGEMENTS

Writing this book was not a solitary task. Successful completion required the cooperation of selected professionals. Each brought their unique talents and invaluable commitment to the project. From the critique of the first sentence until the final publishing details, the author has appreciated these special persons and is grateful for their contributions.

Bonnie Raysdale, Office Manager/Director of Quality Assurance, Children's Services Unit of Methodist Family Services of Philadelphia was instrumental in organizing the original manuscript and completed the early draft. After close review and editing, Lenora H. Milbourne, secretary while I pastored Grace Community United Methodist Church, Chester, Pennsylvania, labored through my corrections to produce the second draft. The final typing and copy-editing were prepared by Debi Kain of A Business Aide in West Chester, Pennsylvania. Thank you all very much.

I am especially thankful to the late Rev. George O. McCalep, Jr., Ph.D., Senior Pastor of Greenforest Community Baptist Church, Decatur, Georgia for his friendship and support. Rev. McCalep was a noted author, founder and president of Orman Press Inc., Lithonia, Georgia. His staff worked tirelessly to prepare **Somebody's Knock-in at Your Door** for publication.

Reverend Dr. Zan W. Holmes Jr., retired Senior Pastor of St. Luke Community United Methodist Church, Dallas, Texas, who serves on the

Board of the United Methodist Publishing House, Nashville, Tennessee, penned the Foreword. His endorsement brings enormous credibility to this book. Dr. Holmes is the narrator for the world acclaimed Disciple Bible Study Videos.

Finally, my sincere appreciation is extended to Suzy Keenan, Director of Communication Ministries for the Eastern Pennsylvania Conference, United Methodist Church. During a single meeting, Suzy's perceptive editorial feedback prompted me to revise the tone in several of the narratives. Respectfully, I take full responsibility for the final product.

Introduction

Somebody's Knock-in at Your Door

Somebody's knock-in at your door,
O sinner, why don't you answer?
Somebody's knock-in at your door.
Knocks like Jesus,
Somebody's knock-in at your door.
Can't you hear him?
Somebody's knock-in at your door.
Answer Jesus,
Somebody's knock-in at your door.
Jesus calls you,
Somebody's knock-in at your door.
Can't you trust him?
Somebody's knock-in at your door.

Harm, by Richard Proulx, b. 1937, Alt., © 1986, GIA Publications, Inc.
African American Heritage Hymnal, 2000

Don't you realize that Jesus is the Somebody who knocks at your door? Our Lord calls to divulge an extremely weighty message. The divine invitation encourages passionate obedience. Accept Salvation. There awaits a fulfilling life in Christ for those who answer the knock with enthusiasm.

"Knock-in" announces that divine intervention seeks to open those inner human doors that are shut to any awakening deep in the sacred core known as the soul. "Knock-in" describes the perpetual action of the Godhead endeavoring to reach souls that cannot or will not entertain the urgent plea. With the echo generated from the exchange between the confronting questions (i.e.; "Can't you trust him?") and the emotionally charged affirmations (i.e.; "Jesus calls you"), "Knock-in" accents to the majesty, power and dominion which God holds over our lives. "Knock-in" conveys the penetrating, persuasive mode of the chosen messenger, Jesus Christ, who intervenes to admonish us about God's promise.

This favorite Negro Spiritual illustrates the call found in Revelation 3:20. Using a repetitive, syncopated beat, Jesus' pleading knock marches through each verse like Ravel's Bolero. The lyric verses are both vivid and riveting. In the musical rendition of this particular text, it is clear that our Lord is the prime mover of the call.

However, when it is stated that God calls, the attribute is not exclusive to any single Person of the Godhead. The work of the call is equally and collectively conveyed in harmony: God – the Father/Creator; God–the Son of God, Redeemer, Jesus Christ, Lord and Savior; as well as God–the Holy Spirit, the Comforter, the Breath of God. God's call is indivisible in unity, acting eternally as one essence and sovereign power. All Persons of the Godhead are significantly present with each knock at the human door.

When any Person of the Godhead elects to lead in any purposeful communication, the targeted individual(s) continues to receive the call in tri-unity. While any Person of the Godhead may act as the principal communicator, the Trinity continues to be inseparable during that contact. All call communications are shared and acted upon inclusively. The cohesiveness of God is never split like a cell during mitosis. Regardless of the strategy which the Godhead chooses, call is delegated in cooperation. Therefore, when Jesus knocks in Revelation 3:20, the Godhead does not leave our Lord to call individuals as a lone ranger.

Advocated in **Somebody's Knock-in at Your Door** is the premise that the Caller communicates with a warm-hearted countenance. This is God accompanying human life in a plethora of endless interventions. This is God authentically showing up in daily life, subliminally instructing, passionately pursuing, and actively changing attitudes and behaviors. This is the Divine Caller purposely orchestrating the environment we inhabit over a lifetime.

The task of answering the call is interwoven among three coordinated factors. The writer refers to these as the three I's. Believers must identify, isolate and intensify. First, identify that at some point in your life, you will be sought after and singled out for a very specific purpose. Then, isolate yourself from the personal interferences which cause you to choose avoidance behavior, by prayerfully reflecting, remembering and replenishing your faith in preparation for a life-renewing journey. Finally, intensify your quiet, sometimes painful discernment, while you actively participate in the visible work which models the Gospel.

Answering the call starts with simply responding to the knock. This is a voluntary decision to accept a new journey as an active member of the Body of Christ. Then, one must honor divine obedience. This requires a spiritual/emotional/psychological mind-set which embraces a commitment to permanently act as a good steward of one's call.

Commitment to one's call is then made up of contrast and lies somewhere among the desire to serve Christ and the Church, a self-giving,

Holy Spirit embodiment which welcomes the peculiar labor of Christian vocation, and a self-forgetting demeanor which approaches ministry regardless of who, what, where or when the call demands. Shrouded in a cloak of faith, the called disciple anticipates being spiritually stretched beyond their imagination. They participate in God's mighty works and deeds with the confidence that call grants them the distinct opportunity to share their sustaining faith with others.

Human beings respond to the call from dissimilar places of faith and vantage points of trust. Theological insights vary. Biblical understanding may be either vast or miniscule. However, there is an overarching promise. The call never ceases. The engaging knock will linger with even greater intensity, whether experienced in a feverish pitch, feeble sound, or deathening silence.

Personal reflection reminds the author that the call is not a popular addition to many people's lives. Sometimes, the divine invitation is treated as an intrusion. The call may cause tension and struggle. You should not dismiss this reality. However, God is merciful in the encounter. It is, indeed, rewarding to work through spiritual unrest and experience the human spirit being lifted beyond the rampant hazards of the human predicament.

While answering the call may be the root of anxiety, we discover satisfaction in the Christian life. The call may cause us to be caught up in a whirl of resistance. Yet, we advance from the childhood of faith to the status of a committed servant.

> A call is never comfortable in the biblical experience. Moses is called to march off into Egypt as part of a two-person invasion of the mightiest nation in the world. Samuel is called to deliver the word of doom to his mentor, Eli. Ruth is called to remain a sojourner in a foreign land.

> Esther is called to risk her position of power and privilege on behalf of those from whom she has come. Jonah is called to go to Nineveh, much to his dismay. Paul is called to recant everything he has been about. Scripture clearly demonstrated to the degree a call becomes comfortable, to that same degree the human agenda has been substituted for God's.[(1)]

A common thread knits the fabric of this book. Amidst our call storms, God never gives us more of a burden than we are able to bear. Our deep, awestruck ponderings are compassionately recognized anticipated by God. As we deal with call anxiety, God is actively supporting and loving us during our struggle. Find confidence in knowing ordinary people are the recipients of this exceptionally noteworthy endorsement.

Chapter I

Somebody's Knock-in at my Door

"Behold, I stand at the door and knock. If one opens, I will come in and sit down side by side with them and sup with them."

—*Revelation 3:20 RSV*

The Prince of Peace Calls

Patiently, Jesus stands outside the door of human, earthly affairs. Our Lord waits pensively like a determined stakeout police officer sternly surveying our vacancy. This is the Savior, knocking to rescue all who stubbornly waste their holy potential. The Redeemer who seeks to reconcile us to harmony with God knocks to promise fellowship. The Prince of Peace calls to free us from our self-imposed solitary lives. This is the Solid Rock attempting to rescue us from the barricades we erect in a futile effort to escape from the call. Like the Laodicean Church, we tend to be unaware of the full measure of blessings guaranteed when we answer the knock and welcome Jesus Christ into our call-ignored lives.

The knock had little or no value to the Laodicean community of faith. The people of Laodicea had a high opinion of themselves. They were self-absorbed in their wealthy system of commerce. A prestigious medical school made them feel protected and privileged.

Because of the successful export/import trade, the Christians of Laodicea also had a false sense of entitlement, which effectively inflated their collective EGO (Ease God Out). Our Lord was not pleased watching them "play" church as opposed to truly being the credible Church. Sadly, they had no idea how Jesus-impoverished and spiritually poor they really were.

Jesus Christ accused the Church of Laodicea of having lukewarm enthusiasm. "Luke-warmness or indifference in religion is the worst temper in the world. If religion is worth anything, it is worth everything. There is no room for neutrality. Christ expects that men [and women] should declare themselves in earnest either for or against Him." (1) "You may avert this last resort to get your attention. Just follow! And obey the call." (2)

In our daily life, our demeanor makes the case. We send mixed messages to visitors who knock at our door. We vacillate between being welcoming and unwelcoming. The entrance to our home may be decorated with beautifully crafted doors. However, they are usually locked and armed with sensitive security systems. Ornate welcome mats express "you are invited to enter." Decorative flowers and plants arranged around the front door suggest "this home is full of warmth. Please come in." Yet, we are not always receptive to the knock at our closed, self-absorbed domain. To be fair, the knock may appear to spell trouble. Call might sound like a threat signal, something to be protected from.

Verbally, we invite people to visit us. When they finally arrive and knock, it is an imposition. Our demeanor reveals our insincerity. The outer-symbols, which signify welcome, are not always genuine. The outer decorations suggest the visitors are welcomed, but once we open the door our cold or lukewarm reception says they are not really wanted or welcomed. While the exterior door paints an inviting picture, entertaining visitors is not a serious commitment from within. Far worst, when visitors suspect we are hidden behind our doors, refusing to answer, they retreat like trespassers, believing they have violated private space. They leave deceived and insulted.

> And so we see the Lord standing at last outside the door of the professing church, and saying so tenderly, 'Behold, I stand at the door and knock: if any one hear my voice, and open the door, I will come in to them, and will sup with them and they with Me.' Ah, beloved friends, it is getting late in the dispensation; the night-shades are fast falling; and the Lord who, in the beginning, was in the midst of His church, stands outside that lukewarm system

which calls itself by His name, and He knocks in vain for entrance! Yet, individuals here and there open to Him, and find His presence is more to them than all else that the earth or the professing church can afford. [(3)]

THE DOOR OPENS ONLY FROM WITHIN

"Artists have depicted the scene with our Lord knocking on a door that does not have any handle on the outside. It can be opened only from within." [(5)] Pennington's reference to artistic renderings of Jesus' knocking on our door intrigues me. I have never had the opportunity to examine these paintings. I am familiar with the work by James Montgomery Flagg. It depicts a similar but earthbound call, the compelling painting; "Uncle Sam Needs You." The knock is heard through the bold, non-verbal voice, which speaks from an inescapably abrupt foreshortened right index finger. That message balloons in Uncle Sam's firm avuncular facial expression and demands compliance through his imposing patriotic attire. The capturing knock does not subside. Forever, you hear it, see it, feel it, and think about it from that moment. In thundering silence, Uncle Sam warns, "there is no time to hedge. You are urgently needed to support the World War effort."

No! is not the preferred answer. The countenance of this hypnotic icon calls for an immediate affirmative decision. The authoritative digital trumpet is pointed at you. It sounds a demand for urgency. As Uncle Sam awakens you, the searching finger provokes a confronted inner consciousness. The dye has been cast. Every segment of the citizenry is called to respond and act with **esprit de corps** (common purpose).

Able-bodied persons who did not volunteer were drafted by the compulsory selective service system. Call has a way of drafting some who will not volunteer. With faith and trust, many men and women found the courage required to make drastic changes in their lifestyle. Allegiance to new vocations became necessary. In these very best and worst of times, Uncle Sam demanded unity. Uncle Sam's digital voice was not a fickle finger of fate which one could escape. It rallied recruits with a bugler's call. Then, there was another effective strategy. During patriotic parades and events filled with religious solemnity, many were compelled to respond. They heard Uncle Sam's message while listening to the peppy militaristic hymnody contained in John Philip Sousa's music.

A CONTINUOUS KNOCK

Why does Jesus continue to knock on the door of our souls? Jesus knocks to alert us that professing Christians are surrounded by spiritual warfare. There is a full-scale battle in the Kingdom of God. Souls must to be saved. Frankly speaking, Jesus needs you!

- It's a genuine heavyweight bout against injustice, insensitivity, and insanity in the social order. You are called to proclaim the Gospel in the release of the captives. "The Spirit of the Lord is upon you." (Isaiah 61:1)
- There is a war between the churched and unchurched children of God. Sometimes it is the churched that resemble the tares and the goats. You are called to "put on the whole armor of God." (Ephesians 6:11)
- Someone must teach the love of Jesus Christ in the midst of social insecurity and social strife. The children of God are called to usher in the spirit of Shalom, which allows "the lamb to lie down with the wolf." (Isaiah 11:6)
- Who will fight for the oppressed, offended, and the outcasted who are ignorant of their rights protected by both the secular

> political system and their power guaranteed by the presence of the Holy Trinity? Christian soldiers are called to carry and live the Cross among the Christ and Holy Spirit starved victims. (Romans 8: 36-39)

Jesus needs you! No time to hedge. Answer the knock and greet the Lord. Our Lord knocks to recruit us. The call evangelizes us to reach out to the least, last and lost. The secular world inhabits a legitimate battlefield. While we are saved by the blood of Christ on Calvary, this war is waged to destroy our safety. Christian vocation, ministry and service, comprise the only human interventions to win the spiritual war. It is a fierce earth vs. heaven campaign. We are called to mend broken lives. As Christians, we should respond to the urgent knock at our soul's door.

Chapter II

Calls to Puzzled Ears

"Therefore Eli said unto Samuel, Go, lie down: and it shall be, if he call thee, that thou shalt say, Speak, Lord; for thy servant heareth. So Samuel went and lay down in his place."

—I Samuel 3:9, KJV

Give me the listening ear. I seek this day the ear that will not shrink from the word that corrects and admonishes–the word that holds up before me the image of myself that causes me to pause and reconsider–the word that challenges me to deeper consecration and higher resolve–the word that lays bare needs that make my own days uneasy, that seize upon every good decent impulse of my nature, channeling into paths of healing in the lives of others.

Give me the listening ear. I seek this day the disciplined mind, the disciplined heart, the disciplined life that makes my ear the focus of attention through which I may become mindful of expressions of life foreign to my own. I seek the stimulation that lifts me out of old ruts and establishes habits which keep me conscious of my self, my needs, my personal interest. *(Howard Thurmond, Printed in; **Prayer in the Black Tradition, The Upper Room**: Nashville, Tennessee, 1987, 80).*

A FAMILIAR VOICE

"Samuel!" The pitch and volume seemed familiar. Clearly, it was his name that was being called. God knew him personally. The convincing call did not subside. Each time, "Samuel" registered with commanding clarity. Samuel responded to his name; however, the call never reached his listening ear. "Samuel", only lodged in his sensory, physical ear.

Eli represented the God-sent voice of authority over Israel. Samuel respected Eli as religious leader, teacher, and surrogate parent. He slept with an ear focused on his physically diminishing, visually challenged geriatric mentor's every move. Mentor and pupil were connected like hand and glove. Eli depended on Samuel for average daily living assistance. The voice and person of the chief priest reigned supreme over Samuel's entire daily life in the Sanctuary at Shiloh.

Duty alerted Samuel. "Eli called me", the lad surmised to himself. In devotion to the old, weary man, Samuel always responded immediately. "I am here; close by and ready to serve you." Somewhat perplexed, Eli stated on three separate occasions, "I did not call you".

Puzzled, Samuel returned to his pallet. Imagine his mental anguish; "Am I dreaming, participating in an illusion or suffering from a serious hearing problem? That sounded exactly like my master. I know his voice." Confusion consumed Samuel's sleepy state of being. He lacked listening ears to awaken him from the clutches of death's counterfeit.

The puzzling confusion was surprisingly easy to explain. Samuel failed to recognize his heavenly Master's voice. After all, he learned to differentiate among the vast meanings of Eli's "Samuel". This particular "Samuel" falsely defined the elder's command, "come quickly, I need you." This was indeed the exact purpose of God's call to Samuel.

A duty-bound lad habitually accommodated his sensory ears to concentrate only on his earthly master's call.

Samuel never consciously heard the voice of God. Identifying audible holy presence eluded him. In defense of this lack of recognition, Samuel writes, "the word of the Lord was precious in those days; there was no open vision (I Samuel 3:16)." The prophet earlier confides that he did not know the Lord, citing the call was never revealed to him (I Samuel 3:7). Physically, young Samuel lived very close, yet spiritually far away from the presence of God.

The Sanctuary at Shiloh afforded Samuel opportunity and motive to access God's call. Israel believed this sacred environment physically housed God. God's presence in the sanctuary was like the hedge which the Holy Spirit keeps around believers. It protected and watched over all believers. Here, Samuel was reared, played, performed his daily chores and practiced the faith among the devout religious community.

Young Samuel's experience was bombarded with viable auditory cues. Either he lived with an undiscipled mind, or God was preparing an unready soul. Listening ears are not attained automatically. They unfold because of daily purposeful conversations with God. Like the passengers on the ill-fated vessel in Adria during the Euroclydon storm, Samuel would have heard only the threat signals contained in the boisterous sea storm. The comforting voice of God in the mist of the turmoil would have been sadly dismissed (Acts 27).

The sanctuary environment amassed a plethora of visual, feeling/touch, tasting and olfactory cues. All were attributed to God's presence during worship, ceremonial feast and religious rites. Perhaps, Samuel was unable to associate these cues with the divine call. Therefore, Samuel was not yet empowered to spiritually hear the knock at his soul. Samuel had essentially little success with listening to God in and around his inherited holy ground experience.

Finally, in the dark, silent solace of the sanctuary floor, Samuel patiently and alertly waited as Eli had advised. At last, he heard God's message in an inspired, instructive communication. No longer was the call interpreted externally "Samuel" in frequency, decibel levels, pitch and volume. The lad heard only God. Eli truly ceased to be his master.

SAMUEL'S CALL

The call of Samuel illustrates several points which seem pertinent to this discussion. These demonstrate that: 1) call seems to operate in human affairs through two somewhat identifiable mediums; 2) call is unpredictable in the manner of its administration and operation and; 3) many children of God struggle to authentically hear their call.

First, Samuel received a secluded call from God. When God imposes direct personal communication or commanding self-imposed action on the soul, this may be described as an intrinsic, inward, private engaging, and heavenly oriented call. God, who resides within the human soul, speaks from inside, where the human mind, emotions and consciousness also finds domicile. It is the goal of divine nature to independently seek out human interior holy potential. Here, any Person(s) of the Triune God may join to kindle interest and shape desires. In this medium, God is not only the sole primary host, but the only influence. H. Richard Niebuhr refers to this experience as the inner persuasive secret call. On three occasions, God communicated to Samuel with this intimate call.

The secret call speaks in a voice which is universally acknowledged and mutually comprehended. The message is commonplace and communicated without losing its meaning because of language barriers. It summons people in all languages such as, but not limited to French, Spanish, Yiddish or Zulu. So universal is this phenomenon, that it most frequently parallels the call stories, and/or call circumstances revealed in Holy Scriptures. Regardless, the recipient's ethnicity, geographic dialect, culture related traditions or religious affiliation, call transcends all human peculiarities.

God also elects to call through people, daily occurrences and significant life circumstances. This mode of communication is facilitated by what is heard, seen, felt or otherwise experienced within the created order. Either overtly or covertly, the extrinsic call utilizes traditions, culture, selected people and specific places or events as chosen vessels to initiate attention to the call.

Extrinsic calls are distinguished as outward, public, sometimes secular externally God motivated earthbound communication. Through this medium, call connects the individual's personal background and daily experience. God continues to be the single primary host, but acts discriminately through divinely inspired secondary host.

Secondary host never act unilaterally of God's direct instruction and presence. These actions may occur consciously or unconsciously; uneventfully and nonspecifically. These earthbound interventions are not accidental nor occur by chance. Secondary host, while divinely empowered, are never capable of altering God's intrinsic or extrinsic strategy. These stewards are intentionally recruited for specific task designated by the Godhead.

Strangely, the ability to attain the listening ear was conceived through the wise extrinsic counsel of a morally feeble religious leader. Eli did not allow his limitation to hamper his secret call to affirm Samuel's intrinsic call. Being an ineffectual leader failed to hinder him during this moment of self-surrender to God's will. Eli was accessible to God's plan to help Samuel realize that his Master called him.

The second point is that Samuel's call occurred unexpectedly. The young lad had not prepared for this sacred moment. Call acted as an expression of God's unceasing activity within the nature of Providence.

The Divine Caller, who is sovereign (the supreme authority) and omnipresent (everywhere simultaneously), planned to personally summon Samuel. Samuel's call demonstrates God's vast versatility. It also explains God's use of dimension.

Dimension generally refers to a standardized method of defining the extent of a body and space that is natural or constructed. It pertains to the measurement of height (i.e.; as an airplane's cruising altitude); width (i.e.; the broadness of a shoe or swimming pool) and depth (i.e.; the deepness of the Atlantic Ocean and Grand Canyon). Two important properties of dimension are scope and magnitude. The latter speaks to the degree or enormity of a place, thing and organized phenomenon in the material universe. Scope relates to range in terms of distance and/or inclusive area. It also designates one's ability to grasp knowledge and resource information.

Even with sincere discernment, discipline or significant spiritual formation, human ingenuity cannot concretely measure, calculate or tangibly comprehend God's transcendent utilization of dimension.

The exact time, actual location, chosen situation, as well as the estimated extend or preferred manner of conferment of call is the sole discretion of the Godhead. Anything and everything necessary to discern, respond to or carryout a specific call resides in the vast wellspring of God's communicated dimensions.

Women, men and children are the involuntary recipients of a call-dimensioned environment. Call-dimensions range from being detailed/graphic to vague/nondescript. Evidence of the very first call-awakening episode is often difficult to determine. It is unclear when or how any dimension of the call will integrate to summon individuals. The answer is in the incomparable, adaptable agency of God.

An interesting contradiction seems to exist in the administration and operation of the call. While God tolerates unbridled freedom to reject the call, those summoned remain obliged to accept the life-long standing invitation. Patiently, God nudges, cajoles, and perhaps pushes and shoves to get attention. The divine will seems committed to let the gift of the free will run its course. Sometimes, without noticeable interference or significant intervention, human choices are honored. Meanwhile, God closely shadows the private human journey.

The final point is that initially Samuel did not recognize the call. After Eli's counsel (I Samuel 3:9), Samuel poised himself to Stop! Look! and Listen! for God's voice. The truth is, with sincere Christian practice and a desire to answer, many struggle to comprehend their call.

Dag Hammarskjold, the Secretary General of the United Nations between 1953-1961, is an example of someone who struggled to comprehend his call. He vaguely alludes to the call to his puzzled ears. In spite of his great wisdom, skill, and perception, he struggled to remember the specifics of his personal call. Hammarskjold could not discern the who, what and when of the divine encounter. The pertinent details of his encounter confused him. One fact is reassuring for everyone. The degree to which an individual is unable to articulate the specifics of his or her call, in no way invalidates the authenticity of active holy presence. What counts is that the Swedish statesman boldly testifies:

> "I don't know who–or what–put the question, I don't know when it was put. I don't even remember answering. But at some moment I did answer Yes! To Someone–or Something – and from that hour I was certain that existence is meaningful and that, therefore, my life, in self-surrender, had a goal." (Dag Hammarskjold, Markings, 1964)

Hammarskjold understood that he was changed. He accepted his new existence which afforded him a peaceful inner solitude. A new unthreatening confidence allowed this Swedish statesman to surrender himself to the holy presence not yet interpreted or significantly revealed. Hammarskjold experienced a call that was not crystal clear. However, an obedient spirit encouraged him to live out that call, knowing that the holy presence sought him out. Likewise, Samuel surrendered immediately to his call. While the call was quite clear and made him uneasy, Samuel obeyed God and declared judgment on Eli's house.

The call is capable of summoning human beings like the slow movement of a steady eddying current flowing through a body of gentle, quiet water. Some are summoned with tender loving care, having uneventfully been nurtured into call readiness over time. For others, the evidence of the call may be inconspicuously insidious. Unaware, they are gradually seduced by divine intervention. There are those who never remember being formally called. They just went. Somehow, some are drawn to the call without hearing the voice of God. Loving the Lord was their testimony. Desiring to serve Jesus Christ constituted their autonomous aspiration. Whether consciously or not, these individuals answered some genuine dimension of the call.

Conversely, a supernatural experience is possible. Noisy calls are commonly reported. Holy presence may arrive in vivid dream-crowded sleep or a perceived cryptic message while wide-awake. People accurately attest to sensational, miraculous incidents and sudden life-changing drama. However administered, and regardless the strategy of operations, the call prevails as an incalculable dimension of divine will.

Call does not guarantee to proceed in one's human history, resembling normally anticipated stages of growth and development. Call is not obliged to follow the usual course of advancing individuals from a general to specific embodiment. The call is not limited to progressing in an orderly sequence during an individual's faith journey. Consider the

Parable of the Laborers (Matthew 20:1-19). Regardless of the manner, medium, intensity or timeliness of dimension, there is no bevy of best ways to be called. All are genuine invitations purposely administered for specific individuals and local congregations.

Everyone experiences their unique discovery of the call. The goal should be to seek "deeper consecration and higher resolve." Be encouraged to accept a disciplined affect as Samuel finally did. Like Dag Hammarskjolds, we may be called to welcome what has been so foreign and unclear; the ever-present message of God. When we humble ourselves to Waiting! Watching! and Wanting!, the dark shadows in our physical. Earthly ears will disappear, and we will discover the light of God's disclosure. Until that appointed moment, know that God continues to yearn for our attention.

Chapter III

Called Into Life

"But when it pleased God, who separated me from my mother's womb, and called me by his grace, to reveal his Son to me, that I might preach…"

Galatians 1:15, KJV

I am created to do something or to be something for which no one else is created; I have a place in God's counsel, in God's world, which no one else has; whether I be rich or poor, despised or esteemed, God knows me and calls me by my name.

God has created me to do some definite service; [God][(1)] has committed some work to me which [God] has not committed to another. I have my mission. I may never know it in this life, but I shall be told it in the next. Somehow I am necessary for [God's] purposes….

I am a link in a chain, a bond of connection between persons. [God] has not created me for nothing. I shall do well; I shall do [God's] work. I shall be an angel of peace, a preacher of truth in my own place, while not intending it, if I do but keep [God's] commandments. *(John Henry Cardinal Newman,* ***Meditations and Devotions.*** *"Hope in God Creator", March 7, 1848)*

Acknowledge Being Called

Human beings are called into life. God granted them authority to superintend in the Kingdom of God on earth. This task was entrusted to human beings through a covenantal relationship in which the Creator has absolute sovereignty. The expectation was that everyone would embrace God's perfect freedom with wise stewardship.

Natural selection motivated man and woman to achieve the standing biped position. Erect posture influenced a curiosity for an expanded world-view. Subsequent development of the upper extremities accounted for an abundance of intricate fine and gross motor functions. Greater utilization of hand-eye coordination enhanced problem solving. Advanced adaptive behavior skills brilliantly surfaced. Man and woman quickly learned to adjust to the challenges of multi environmental stimuli. Through millions of years of evolution, humanity was blessed with a remarkable brain. This magnificent organ facilitated high levels of cognition, abstract thinking, inventive tool making and incredible multi-sensory perception.

These God-given endowments promoted interest to live a complex lifestyle, which is highlighted by a gregarious culture and sophisticated aesthetic awareness. People participate in a complex political society. They possess articulate speech, along with intricate systems of signs, symbols and expressive body language.

This distinction was not earned. It must never be misconstrued as an inherited birthright to greatness. The elite status was not a reward for any merited deeds. Because of God's benevolent act of mercy toward human beings, they do not receive what is truly deserved. And due to God's sufficient grace which overcomes for their imperfection, the unmerited privileged status is proof that human beings have been the recipients of much that is undeserved.

From the beginning of God's Creation, man and woman emerged as the central object of God's divine love. God carefully monitored and enabled human potential. Our purpose was to acknowledge being chosen vessels. We are called to nurture people's needs until Jesus returns in full glory. When one responds to the call, he/she voluntarily begins an intentional journey to achieve who/what God originally called them to pursue.

Heredity and Environment Prepare One for The Call

God called me into life. Mother and Dad were chosen to conceive and rear me. I was invited to evolve into God's purpose from the composite of heredity and environment. These are the determinates which harmoniously cooperated to define who I am, was and will be in the future. Together, these are the interacting influences which make up my basic identity. Heredity and environment collaborate to shape adaptive behavior necessary for daily encounters. Subsequently, my hereditary endowment in a specified locus, functions to teach me how to order life among rest/sleep, work/play, privacy/fellowship and learning/application, all in preparation to become call-ready.

Like you, I am created from the original common stock, Adam and Eve, the progenitors of all human life as interpreted in the Creation Story in the Book of Genesis. On the other hand, it was God's will to call me into life from a vastly diverse people and be specifically of Negroid origin. My ethnicity is perfect for my specific call journey. Guess what? Equally, so is yours. We basically share common ground. The Creator chose us "as is" to be who we are, wherever we are called to journey.

With 80% water, 16% oxygen, an assortment of minerals and chemical compounds, human beings were formed from the dust of the earth.

Notice, God did not mold them from fertile agricultural soil. Finely granulated gold nor the powdered particles of diamonds scattered in the belly of rock formation were ever options. God selected ashes, the trampled, wind blown vestige from fertile soil to sculpt our protoplasmic framework.

Understand, God foreknew the human body would dwell in the humble carcass of such irrelevant matter. The genotype (hereditary traits) of God's children would nestle in a pauper's cloak of skin and bony skeleton, then be influenced throughout life by their phenotype (human interaction with the environment). The divinely inspired combination was all God's idea.

During their loving union, Frederick, Sr., and Arlena, transmitted their genetic profile. I inherited their genes. Theirs became mine. This was the shared, invisible and personalized blueprint God called them to design. Consequently, I became a reasonable facsimile of my parents, but not a carbon copy. God invented Frederick, Jr. to become only himself, to serve in the ministry for only God. Everything about me is a component of my call. Likewise, this applies to you.

Everyone has a story which is the foundation of their particular call. I was the first of six children, three brothers and two sisters. A healthy balance describes our rearing. Mother and Dad respected their children's individual differences. Valuing an education and developing a work ethic were encouraged. Emphasis centered on participation in a wide variety of organized youth activities. My childhood may be described as stable and rewarding. In retrospect, the experiences, traditions and framework for reasoning learned during my home life significantly influenced the manner in which I would interpret the call.

My parents supported a religious posture, which proclaimed Jesus Christ as Lord and Savior. They expected adherence to the moral conduct which reflected the Ten Commandments as a basis for daily living. A practical theology centered around the, "Golden Rule" (Matthew 7:12). Dad's major theme incorporated the importance of self-worth and respect for others. I continue to hear him state, "You're no better than anyone else and no one else is better than you."

While Mother is United Methodist, Dad is an Episcopalian. Having been baptized and confirmed in the Episcopal Church, I came to appreciate the religious ceremony and solemn reverence of that tradition. However, I was blessed that my acquaintance with Methodism afforded me an accentuated understanding of the Holy Spirit as an instrument of God's grace. This richness became evident as I witnessed the Methodist denomination's emphasis on evangelism through music and preaching. I vicariously experienced the Wesleyan class system as a lad, from the stair-steps of both my home and my grandmother's apartment. With a smile, I shall never forget the lump in my throat after my first impromptu "Amen" during worship.

LIFE BUILDERS NURTURE A SPIRITUAL METAMORPHOSIS

My Corner, Seventh & Edward Streets in Chester, Pennsylvania, is the first physical location God placed me. I arrived on the day of my birth in my maternal grandparent's bedroom. The Messiah inherited Bethlehem. Solomon was the heir of Davidic royalty. In God's infinite wisdom, I received My Corner. It would become the focal point of many significant events and life building lessons during my childhood and early adult life.

Here, Booker T. Washington Elementary School and Frederick Douglas Junior High School would nurture the formative years of my education. Directly across the street, Saint Mary's Episcopal Church effectively functioned as my church community until age thirty-eight. Three hundred feet down Seventh Street, you could find me deeply immersed in activities at the West Branch YMCA. I claim this corner in the precious name of Jesus Christ. In retrospect, the teachings of my assigned urban asphalt turf are prominently stamped in and on me. My Corner never shortchanged me in preparing for the call. In fact, I am indebted to My Corner. Sometimes, I failed to live up to its enduring Christ-filled standards.

A bit of irony exists relative to the location of my birth and the local institutions which physically approximate My Corner. This small parcel of urban terrain taught me the three R's; perfected my talents for music and athletics; started me on my Christian journey, thereby awakening me to appropriate social behavior and moral responsibility. Within this scant space in God's massive creation, young Frederick, Jr. progressed in academic, religious, and social-emotional development. My Corner represents one of God's earliest gifts to me. It was meant to be an extremity of divine presence.

Even now, the Seventh & Edward Streets inheritance raises its glorious head in me. At this very moment, it rushes throughout my arteries and pumps in my heart to inform my daily decisions. Sometimes, it's like the fire that Jeremiah proclaims is shut-up in his bones. I recognize the pulse of My Corner rhythmically moving me into action. Both covertly and overtly, my senses are acutely aware of its faithful vigil, as I discern my entry into chartered and uncharted territory. Constantly, I glean My Corner's network of valuable cues to hear God's voice as only I am called.

Location is paramount in determining the value of real estate. My Corner is the priceless prime property God willed me. Seventh & Edward Streets is not physically impressive or historically noteworthy. Neither should it be characterized as invaluable sprawl. Occasionally, I have paid a higher price for admission into society because this corner represents my roots. Sadly, it is true. Hailing from "Nazareth" caused me unwarranted visibility to the Nathaniel's of the world (John 1:46). However, God always prevailed in leveling the playing fields. Like the lilies of the valley, My Corner, withstood the test of time in me, standing unbended and conquering social obstacles with an enduring posture which was never broken by the raging winds which occasionally accosted me.

Three years after my birth, my parents purchased the home in which they reside today. It is a ten-minute walk from My Corner. What is imprinted in my mind are the many names and faces of Seventh & Edward Streets and the home up the hill. They were family/neighbors, white and blue collar, male/female, of different political and religious orientations. Some were God-sent messengers and tremendous role models. Others functioned as stumbling blocks hired by satan to rebuff me, to sabotage the Christ-awareness embedded in me.

I shall never forget the lessons incorporated within these experiences. They influenced my understanding about Christ in and among other people. There was Mr. Darney Belgrave; my trombone teacher during grades 3-12. A native of Barbados, he migrated to America and became very active in the Salvation Army music ministry. Mr. Belgrave not only exposed me to my musical gifts but also opened my eyes to African heritage in the Scriptures. Sometimes, these sessions after practice were much more intriguing.

Saint Mary's was a boon to my early interest in ordained ministry. This congregation was also a valuable training ground for life in general. Mr. John F. Reason, the Director at the West Branch YMCA always lectured about, "Creating, Maintaining, and Extending," self in meaningful Christian goals. What was boring then is often blended into my pastoral advice to young people today. I learned the lessons of My Corner well.

Then, there was Moses Lermann, the Russian Jew, who paid me for odd jobs in his variety store. For some strange reason, he enjoyed talking to me about the Jewish socio-religious culture and the Hebrew God he referred to as Yahweh. Moses always captured my attention. My old friend probably never had a clue that he was a part of the extrinsic witnesses whom God had chosen to help me hear the call.

Miss Murray and Miss Ricks seemed to cross my path constantly in public school, church life, the city recreation department, and special excursions for children. How can I ever forget Mrs. Emma Brinkley, my first guidance counselor, who told me, "Frederick, God has given you gifts to become almost whatever you want to." I thank God for, Miss Clara DeShields, my history teacher who insisted, "you need not talk like Porky Pig." Diligently, she encouraged me to believe I could overcome my speech impediment. Her diligence paid off. I continue to recall her tears of joy when I spoke at my junior high school graduation ceremonies.

In retrospect, it was during my junior high school years that I became acquainted with some inkling of the call. God's presence initially emerged as a warm nature/nurturing effect. A humbling feeling surrounded me. I always felt protected from the ills of urban life. This reassuring warmth covered me like grandmother's old patchwork quilt. God seemed tactile and physically embracing. The decisively speaking God with the secret/private call was unknown to me at this time. Oddly enough, the idea of becoming a minister/priest continued to take shape in my young mind. A peculiar sense of specialness helped me to believe my thoughts were appropriate.

This was my season of new enlightenment. A spiritual metamorphosis had begun. My base-line cognition of God provided me a host of matching experiences which further sharpened my interest in ordained ministry. I recall:

- The number of adults who suggested that ordained ministry suited me. This vocation was affirmed for me by others. I guess we may surmise that the extrinsic voice of God was actively engaging me.
- The fact that I never had to be prompted to attend church and participate in its activities. I truly enjoyed the local congregation atmosphere.
- The curious manner in which I would listen to Bible study through the mail slot of my grandmother's house. I did not want to be present, but always wanted to hear the Word. Sometimes, I would allow myself to be detected by the adults.
- The serious manner in which I would play preacher and/or administer Holy Communion in my backyard to any friend who would sit still long enough to appease me.
- The manner I quietly scrutinized my priest and other pastors. I was fascinated by Rev. Barbour's right-eyed monocle. Rev. Scott's ability to engage his congregation always consumed me. I was blessed to see two pastors cry, and I recalled these pastors when I was provoked to tears.

Today, I believe that God's call was vigorously establishing communication with me, presenting its full reality, touching my destiny by fulfilling all of my Christian experiences. I savor those convincing moments when singing with the Boy Scout gospel choir; playing Swing Low Sweet Chariot as a concerto with the school band and **Ave Maria** on my trombone at church programs. While being an acolyte was so cleansing for my boyish, naughty nature, the activity also gave me a front seat to learn every detail of Father Miller's movement during worship. Early, I committed to memory much of the Book of Common Prayer.

Through it all, I was unconsciously clinging to a Christian value I had learned to trust. The foundation was laid without my knowledge or permission. The Caller just worked around my will. During the next three decades, my will would vacillate. The desire to answer increased. The tug-of-war between "yes" and "no" mercifully subsided and granted me peace.

Before answering the call, God permitted me to pursue my vocational choice of physical therapy and teaching in the area of exceptional populations. I sincerely believe God placed Mr. Jack, Lacy, and Rudolph in my early life to stimulate interest in challenged citizens at risk. While the former had a complete left upper extremity amputation, the latter two endured frequent grand mal seizures and moderate mental retardation (Downs Syndrome), respectively. Mr. Jack impressed me with his artistry in adapting to average daily living demands with just one arm. There was no task he could not perform.

I always attempted to convince my friends to include Lacy and Rudolph in our adolescent play. I employed creative ideas and suggested augmented rules to accommodate their opportunity to join us. Sometimes my playmates rejected these changes. Today, I recall Mr. Jack, Lacy and Rudolph as "angels" in disguise who revealed the expectations of Christ to me at a very tender age. The lessons acquired while sharing their season in my life resonates with the Gospel.

Through it all, grace abounded for me. During conception, grace surrounded mom, dad, and me, the micro-minuscule zygote they produced. Grace followed me before I was aware of the divine invitation. Grace prevailed and was steadfast in my darkest moments. Finally, I became privy to the fact that, through grace, God overcame for me, and graciously introduced me to the knowledge of Christ and faith in my call.

After answering the call, I succumbed to a habit. A major challenge would be to look occasionally at the series of my childhood photographs and ask, "Does the person you see truly resemble who God 'Called Into Life?' Have I become a reasonable facsimile of whom God intended? Or, am I only a partial representative of the experience My Corner provided?"

Like me, you are the only one of you whom God has Called Into Life and invited to claim your own unique personhood. God factors in all of the adventures, traditions, results of your human interactions, along with the composite of your genetic, environmental, and coincidental life to form a gestalt of who/whose we are called to be. You may be an identical twin or have a striking look-alike, but no one has your specific call–only you. This is your story. Find the voice to sing your song and walk in the footsteps which you have been called to trod.

Go down memory lane. Recall your starting place. Embrace the journey with the harmoniously integrated nature (heredity) and nurture (environment) God dealt you. Whether good, unpleasant or indifferent, this is the hand the Almighty has chosen to deal you. Accept your gift. Because of your one-of-a-kind inheritance, God has assured that the gospel will be passed on.

Chapter IV
Know That You Are Known

"This word of the Lord came to me: 'Before I formed you in the womb I chose you, and before you were born I consecrated you; I appointed you a prophet to the nations.' Ah! Lord God,' I answered, "I am not skilled in speaking; I am too young.' But the Lord said, 'Do not plead that you are too young; for you are to go to whatever people I send you, and say whatever I tell you to say."

— Jeremiah 1:4-7, REB

"I am the good Shepherd, and know my sheep, and am known of mine."

—John 10:14, KJV

PRE-ORDAINED TO ANSWER THE CALL

At the moment of conception, parents are chaperoned by the holy presence of the Holy Spirit. The Holy Spirit presided when Mary conceived our Incarnate Lord. God personally intervened to bless Sarah and Abraham in their geriatric years with the promised conception of Isaac. While in utero, the foreordained embryonic John the Baptist was filled with the Holy Spirit at the announcement of the coming Messiah, his cousin, Jesus. It is inconsistent for a loving God to be apart from God's children during any time in their human history.

Like Isaac, Samuel, and John the Baptist, you and I are the offspring of chaperoned parents. Before conception God knew us. We were set-aside long before befriending our call. A God with flawless insight called us to be self-giving servants for something special. The goal was for us to find satisfaction in roles as self-forgetting disciples. God never doubted that we would eventually participate in good works. When God blessed our conception, an intimate, hands-on relationship commenced to draw us closer to the call.

Predestined? No, not in the sense that we have been divinely decreed to heaven or hell; automatically relegated to behaviors of wheat or tares; predetermined to lots of either boon or bain life chances. Predestined? Yes, God knew us before our physical birth. We were preordained to answer the call and participate in some individualized prescribed work of Jesus Christ. An omnipotent and omnipresent God was resolute about our potential and started preparing for our call journey in advance. Is this not what parents and families do when the news of an expected baby is announced by the doctor? We constantly remained in the Creator's utmost favor. Loved ones hustle with excitement to get ready for the unborn child. God declared, with a sovereign made up mind that we were worth being members of the Body of Christ.

> "All people are seen as created in the image of God. This creative energy of God, this ability to bring form out of chaos, is given to all people, who in turn are instructed to be fruitful. People are made co-creators with God, to continue the creative process, to have a part in completing the building of the earth". (1)

It follows that all human life is cherished and celebrated. Therefore, our birth did not provoke God. No one constitutes surplus population. Fortunately, it is impossible to surprise God with an unexpected arrival. Everyone has an established reservation with an accompanying guaranteed confirmation of arrival date. A place has been prepared for us to assist in ordering the earth with the Gospel.

When God elected to create us, no mistakes were committed. An all-knowing Almighty was incapable of making any errors. Our natural imperfections were not the result of divine carelessness. Every planned detail was accurately scrutinized. Expected outcomes materialized when we were formed in the womb. Only our answer to the universal call awaited. Time remained on God's side.

Economy of time and labor did not foster omissions or shortcuts in our highly structured anatomical and physiological function. God never considered us trial models created during some precipitous selection process. Before entering mother's womb, it was decided who and whose we would be. God promptly claimed us. Eternally, we would be lovingly nurtured by the possessive nature of this sovereign God.

Furthermore, nothing was spared from the rich treasure chest of God's unfathomable gift of fellowship. In a protective act to oppose the chaos of our rampant free will, God consecrated us. Human beings were made holy. Excellence prevailed in spite of instinctive shortcomings. Specificity was achieved with efficient planning and sufficient foresight.

Oden[4] reminds us that God chooses to give us the extraordinary gift of finite freedom, that carries with it the possibility of abuse…The fact that God created human beings is clear evidence that God wished to have some part of creation to share to some degree God's own infinite freedom, power and goodness.

God knows us. Jones explains that "know" has the same overtone as "elect" or "choose." Likewise, "I consecrate you" expresses the idea of separation from worldly ambitions to the purpose and service of God. [2]

> "Holiness can be a property, like clean or unclean, and it can be related to ethical activity and spiritual dedication, but the term assumes that what God designates as holy is reserved for (i.e., set apart for) a particular task. Otherwise said, God's choice of Jeremiah, his designation of him as prophet, is the reason he is sanctified. It is not the other way around, as if Jeremiah's moral and spiritual attributes are the impetus for God's selection of him as prophet." [3]

Jeremiah heard God in a direct and definitive call. In response, he pointedly expressed several reasons why he failed to qualify for the awesome invitation. Such a self-condemning defense was all for naught. A pre-decided God resolved that Jeremiah met call standards long before inhabiting the earth. Operating astutely, divine foresight equipped Jeremiah with the appropriate "everything" necessary to carry out his specific call.

Just like you and me, Jeremiah responded to the call with alarm. Momentarily, he forfeited his ability to be holy. The mammoth assignment left him awestruck. "This is out of my league; I cannot handle it". Being the chosen voice seemed to be the task for an expert. Jeremiah's suspect background credentials made him feel incompetent to adhere to what the commissioning required. A career in prophetic service generated little passion. Reluctance crowded his demeanor. Believing he was suitable proved to be difficult. The idea of confronting multitudes of religiously indifferent, ethically defiant sinners signaled trouble.

As you might expect, God never indulge excuses. My mother's retort seems appropriate. When attempting to get off the hook for something I opposed doing, she would simply say, "excuses do not explain; explanations are not understood." Excuses and explanations were very human responses to what appeared as quite a formidable request of Jeremiah. The called prophet felt disarmed. The notion of being involuntarily appointed to certain failure threatened his comfort zone. The call demanded that Jeremiah travel to foreign territory. "God, you did not consider my background and experience. I have glaring deficiencies. Re-examine my resume and you will agree," was the substance of Jeremiah's reply.

So, when God directed Jeremiah, "Go to whatever people I send you, and say whatever I tell you to say", it was not a scolding voice. An affirming God was essentially saying, "Jeremiah, you are able to do this. I expect you to succeed. I have confidence in you because I consecrated you for this purpose. You possess a significant portion of my holiness. When people see you act, listen to you speak, they should experience something of me in you. You are a mirror reflection of my purpose. Go!, prophesize among the people of the earth."

Being known by God means: when you are lost and cannot hear, you count. When you hear and are too busy to fulfill your responsibility to God, you count. You count because God never gives up on you. You count because God was serious about calling you into life and inviting you to fulfill your purpose on earth. Divine love values you enough to pursue you continuously. Divine love will eventually turn you around and cause you to face your call.

This should be a satisfying comfort, which ultimately leads us to respond:

> *"Here I am, Lord; it is I, Lord*
> *I have heard you calling in the night.*
> *I will go, Lord, if you lead me.*
> *I will hold your people in my hand."* [5]

Chapter V

Experience Counts

"I was no prophet, neither was I a prophet's son; but I was a herdsmen, and a gatherer of sycamore fruits: and the Lord took me as I followed the flock, and he said unto me, Go, prophesy unto my people."

Amos 7:14,15, KJV

You cannot know God until you've stopped telling yourself that you already know God. You cannot hear God until you stop thinking that you've already heard God.

I cannot tell you My Truth until you stop telling Me yours. ***(Neal Donald Walsch,* In Conversations With God, *book I, 8.)***

APPROPRIATE EXPERIENCE

The approximate date was 767-753 B.C. It was the overlapping era of Uzziah, King of Judah, and Jeroboam, the son of Joash, King of Israel. During these reigns, "there was pride (Amos 6:13-14), plenty, and splendor in the North land, elegance in the cities, and might in the palaces. The rich had their summer and winter palaces adorned with costly ivory (Amos 3:5), gorgeous couches with damask pillows (Amos 3:12) on which they reclined at their sumptuous feasts. They planted pleasant vineyards and anointed themselves with precious oils" (Amos 6:46, 5:11). (1)

Externally, the Northern Kingdom of Israel painted a portrait of prosperity. Worship was practiced in a pious manner. Annual tithes were offered punctually in the sanctuaries. However, internally moral decay festered at the core of its' very soul. Social misconduct dominated the citizens. An acquired pattern of behavior conditioned Israel to murmur rebelliously against God. Irreligious practice displaced sacred traditions. Self-serving sacrifices insulted their Hebrew heritage. "There was no justice in the land (Amos 3:10), the poor were afflicted, exploited, even sold into slavery (Amos 2:6-8,5:11), and the judges were corrupt (Amos 5:12)".(2)

Material wealth was gained on the backs of the underclass. The marginalized incurred oppression at the hands of the political strategy. The privileged class profited from a structured economic system, which made the rich richer, while the poor endured increased poverty. Irreligious inclinations caused the ruling class to abandon all conventional wisdom. Stubborn minds did not pay attention to the admonishing Word of God. God needed one who had the appropriate experience to address the nation.

While tending his flock, Amos enters into deep mediation. He later testifies that he was swiftly captured by the Spirit of the Living God. As opposed to a refreshing experience of God enabling a thriving community of faith, the plagues of the grasshoppers, fire and the plumb line (Amos 7:1-9) revealed judgment and punishment against Israel.

Apprehended and purposely diverted from his normal, habitual duties, Amos was petitioned by God to pursue the human flock, to prune the dying branches attached to the Vine (John 15: 1-8). The preferred candidate for this appointed time never said, "No!"

God called Amos, an example of the salt of the earth, to apprise the Northern Kingdom of their impending doom. An unknown citizen from the perceived inferior Southern Kingdom, who cultivated figs, the cheap crop of the desert orchids, carried the burden of calling the nation to repent. Amos experience as a sheepherder and fruit grower had enormous value in fulfilling for God's plan for the Northern Kingdom. A background of poverty had purpose toward bringing Israel into account.

The rural peasant, without apology, informed Ahaziah, the high priest of his scant qualification. Amos felt his credentials were rooted in an obscure background.

> We can assume from the conversation (with Ahaziah, the high priest) that Amos did not attend the school of prophets or receive training from other prophets. He seemed to have been called by God and prepared for his unique mission by experience and special revelations. In Amos, we see the profile of a common man called by God to carry a special message.[3]

Hard evidence does not support that Amos was blessed with any particular entitlement for a career in prophetic ministry. He was not privileged to study at the feet of a religious scholar as young Saul experienced with Gamaliel. Nor, was he privy to Samuel's fate. Before birth Samuel's mother, Hannah, offered him to receive the tutelage of Eli, the high priest. Scripture does not reveal that the would-be prophet received prolonged preparation with God, as did Moses.

Amos graduated from the school of hard knocks. He was an astute student of poverty who survived with honors. Attentively, he sat at the feet of irreligious politics. As he admonished the Northern Kingdom about the triadic sin of injustice, oppression and greed, Amos had already inhabited the text and topic he preached. Social degradation and economic strife constituted major chapters in his autobiography.

So, when Amos states, "Neither was I a prophet's son," the native Teokan ascribes to a higher, more ecclesiastical relationship. Perhaps, Amos was declaring that God's choice of him was not grounded in his genetic endowment, earthly parental guidance or social context, but rest in a heavenly authority in which only God prevailed. Amos believed he was primarily–a child of God. For him, this appointment denoted devotion to divine parentage. Amos believed his call evolved in a heavenly genealogy. Amos' call constituted the ultimate experience under the reign and supervision of God.

Mercifully, Amos reached out to Israel with liberating love and genuine compassion. Memories of his meager existence did not reduce him to anger. Amos served the hostile population with sensitive judgment and long-suffering.

Experience prompted Amos to abhor corruption. However, his humbling experience with God enabled him to let forgiveness surface. The power of upper-class prejudice failed to threaten his charismatic temperament. So, when Amos cried, "let judgment run down as waters and righteousness as a mighty stream" (Amos 5:24), he spoke as if he commanded a holy river to descend upon Israel and instantly cleanse both oppressor and the oppressed which his prophetic message embraced.

Amos experienced God as being pertinent in every aspect of his personal life. Experience with God included not only the subjective world of sensory and physical phenomenon, but more especially, an objective world which encouraged theological reflection expressed in rational thought and understood because of biblical teachings.

"Amos' experience of God is shaped by his view of life – in the perspective of a rural peasant, a powerless victim chosen by a God of justice."(4) "The way we experience God is shaped by the way we define God. A narrowly limited view of God results in a narrow, inadequate life of the spirit. Amos has a lot to say about what kind of God our God is. The relationship of people to God is shaped by their relationship to each other."(5)

> God gives us experience. Why are you a follower of Jesus Christ? How is it that you are a praying [person], and a worshiping [person], and a believing [person]? Why aren't you a scoffer, or a cynic, or one of those thousands completely unmoved by any kind of religion? Are you not in tune with all this strangeness of God's call from the fact that he called you to follow him? We haven't grasped the nature of our faith till we have pondered the fact that we did not choose it all ourselves, but God chooses us. God's choice of us was real experience.(6)

Experiencing God is essential to possessing an understanding of one's call. Knowing God personally is actualized through learning to share in others joy/sadness, jubilation/tribulations, famine/plenty, question/concerns, repentance and forgiveness. When the Holy Spirit travels with us, as with Amos, to touch human life, we come to identify with those we serve. Many times, we have worn similar shoes, and walked near identical paths. We find our experiences are tied and linked together with others. In "giving and receiving", giving to neighbors by the will of God and receiving empowerment from God, we share experience.

The experience of a quiet naturalist could not succumb to the volleys of violently sinful people. His rebuke, while seemingly harsh, was grounded in an experience of merciful acts of caring. Amos understood his newly acquired double consciousness: serving a perfect God, while attending to the needs of grossly imperfect Israel. Amos felt real pain for Israel's sinful plight. He was aware that God was not pleased with the nation's moral misbehavior and spiritual dysfunctional attitude. Amos' heart was of a servant that accepted God's concern as his very own.

With a determined countenance, Amos pursued the citizenry. With a penetrating message adorned with language filled with illustrative hymnic poetry, he challenged a society that was complacent and helplessly connected to a sacredly hollow lifestyle. His was a fresh breath of inspiration for the faithful few of the Northern Kingdom during these distressful days. Experience never allowed Amos to separate from God nor the children of God.

While God enhanced his persona, Amos continued to think like a farmer. He maintained the effect of a quiet country dweller. First hand, Amos witnessed how a few diseased sheep could destroy an entire flock, while several rotten figs caused sycamore trees to die. Prayerfully, Amos applied that experience to the decaying state of affairs in Israel. Experience compelled Amos to express the truths of the Word and the outreaching nurture of agape (love).

Also, Amos had participated in the miracle of birth. He heard the doleful wail of a newly born ewe as it struggled. Giving attention to dying lingered in his memory. To him, Israel needed immediate care to save its dying soul. He witnessed Israel's apparent demise before his very eyes. Amos administered spiritual first aid and treatment in his message. He offered total rehabilitation for sinful Israel by advising repentance.

Amos tackled this prophetic mission with brute force. Wrestling with recalcitrant souls typified the task of corralling aggressive, run-away sheep. For Amos, working diligently to excise the unproductive behaviors and attitudes of coarse sacrilegious human life resembled the pruning of the dead branches from a tree which obviously continued to have potential to bear fruit in a newly transformed life.

A rugged outdoorsman, Amos maintained his prophetic goals regardless of the weather conditions. He braved the natural weather elements. Non-stop, he preached God's Word. He roamed the countryside, paced through the marketplaces, traveled during all seasons and camped out at the gates of the rich and powerful. God accessed Amos' rigorous experience, the fortitude and endurance necessary to survive the dusty storms of Tekoa. With inate courage, Amos weathered the storms of the religious leaders and politicians. With a patient countenance, he waited for the peaceful aftermath of repentant souls. The experience of a resilient herdsman and committed farmer for all seasons would be God's voice in Israel twenty-four hours a day, seven days weekly.

This ordinary villager who possessed mental and physical stamina was revived during his deep meditative experience with God. So, when Israel blatantly avoided him and scattered like lost sheep, Amos persevered. Amos tirelessly committed to gather the lost souls. The herdman continued to love the deviants during his admonishing round up, always demanding they return to the Shepherd, the God of Israel.

Amos understood how grazing sheep often nibbled themselves away from green pastures and became lost in dry, dusty desert conditions. Sadly, the grass, for some, looks greener beyond the safety with God. It was as if Amos was familiar with the Christ of Luke 15 who compassionately searches for every lost sheep until they are found.

SECOND CAREER PERSONS

Scholarship, apprenticeship and internship; inheritance coupled with family background; diploma, degree; time-in-grade or on-the-job training; age, gender, ethnicity; union certification and occupational licensure; resume, reference, along with established reputation: these are a bevy of treasured trophies we value. We erroneously believe these are essential human qualifiers. With these earned credentials we claim confidence in what we can do. With these, we declare our right to passage into personally chosen careers, vocations or professions. It is self-validating to secure position based on documented sweat from one's own brow. Being qualified is deemed paramount if one is to access the entitlements of life, liberty and the pursuit of happiness.

Second career persons are often considered naturals for responding to God's call. The general assumption persists that their former vocational skills and training have automatic carry-over value. Previous professional credentials sustain their future call. The popular perception stresses that these attributes may be re-tooled. Also, the suggestion prevails that second career person's expertise satisfies God's purpose after they accept the call.

A nurse with a proven, compassionate bedside manner does not automatically translate into proficiency during hospital visitation ministry. A prison guard is not promised to be effective in prison ministry. Success in Christian education is not preserved in the methods and techniques of a public school teacher. Professors adept at public speaking and lecturing, are not necessarily endowed to be soul-stirring preachers.

Good works in past professions are not exclusive qualifiers to glorify God. Good works should not be expected to achieve God's favor in the future. Some professional experience may never be accepted by God to assist in their call. Because these talents may lack experience as related to God, their functions corrupt God's present plan. These past gift-laden talents remain the root of human will and does not reflect the will of Christ.

Reflection on Neal Donald Walsch's quote at the beginning of this narrative bears much merit. It offers food for thought. Human beings (i.e.; second career persons) will never know God's new revelation if they continue to hold on to yesterday's treasured trophies for today's call. Knowing God is impossible if the called children of God insist on re-cycling skills, education and training. The Call usually requires their faith to utilize new, divinely inspired experiences to disregard old habits. New experiences may initially cause discomfort; however, the faithful individual will confidence to do God's will.

Amos clearly experienced the love of God which granted him and Israel alike forgiveness. Because of real religious experience, Amos knew God objectively through the traditions of his practiced Jewish faith. God enabled Amos to live this experience. If the daily life experience of a shepherd and fruit grower had carry-over value, it existed because Amos was able to discern the difference between the message of God and the data from his past professions.

Experience Counts seems to suggest that Amos was a second career person who gravitated toward old vocational skills. The fact is, God validated Amos' personhood (i.e.; character, resilience, fortitude and compassion). Amos was enabled because he carried over a believer's conviction that experienced life as it only related to God. The identical attributes he depended on before the call, now fortified him as legitimate ingredients for the vocation of prophet. The treasured skills of the past never separated Amos from God's redeeming purpose.

Chapter VI

Called to Vocation

"I therefore, the prisoner of the Lord, beseech you that ye walk worthy of the vocation wherewith ye are called."

Ephesians 4:1 RSV

The kind of work God usually calls you to is the kind of work (a) that you need most to do and (b) that the world most needs to have done. If you really get a kick out of your work, you've presumably met requirement (a), but if your work is writing TV deodorant commercials, the chances are you've missed requirement (b). On the other hand, if your work is being a doctor in a leper colony, you have probably met requirement (b), but if most of the time you're bored and depressed by it, the chances are you have not only bypassed (a) but probably aren't helping your patients much either. [1]

PURSUIT OF LASTING FULFILLMENT

"What do you want to be when you grow up?" Implied is the notion that an individual prepares for labor force readiness by independently choosing a profession or trade. Suggested is the idea that cultivating a vocation is a personal responsibility. "When you grow up" seems to indicate it is expected human behavior to, somehow, acquire a socially accepted work ethic. Presumed is the future acquisition of a double consciousness goal: successfully satisfying basic needs (i.e.; food, shelter, clothing), and proactively having the ability to court mainstream occupational trends.

To varying degrees, this pressing question enters everyone's thoughts about vocational goals. Some carry the burden throughout a lifetime. In the quest to find a satisfying answer to this scrutinizing inquiry, many incur hardship. At the center of this prominent ordeal is a false assumption. The presupposed notion is we have exclusive autonomy to decide what is best for us.

This burdensome interrogation proceeds to press conscious thought at an early age. Children imitate occupations that they view favorably. They mimic the vocational functions noted during daily experiences. Manufactured toys heighten interest. Halloween costumes depict preferred vocations. Wearing these particular costumes, children resemble the miniature adult-like portraits created by Henri Rousseau, the late 1800's French painter. The message states "This is what I want to do and look like when I grow up."

Life circumstances have an impact. For instance, the events of 9/11 influenced children to aspire to vocations such as police officers, EMT specialist, or firefighters. They are fascinated and encouraged with the professions characterized by their television sheroes and heroes. Entertainers, athletes, lawyers/judges, teachers, or gourmet chefs seem to be viable persons to emulate. Consider this candid talking point. How much does Christian education programming (i.e.; Sunday School, Christian camping, drama, youth events) excite children to embrace the lasting conviction, "When I grow up, I want to be just like Jesus?"

The rush to attain "somebodiness" looms heavily on the heart of late adolescent/young adults. It is important to establish status among peers and the larger society. As the search for a meaningful vocation intensifies, greater tension often ensues. Personal meaning and validation are attached to attaining fame and fortune. On a more basic level, the quest for a proper fit with a profitable vocation is tied to the normal human drives for survival and security.

During my tenure as a college professor, I encountered scores of students who had struggled with this foreboding question. Eventually they became frustrated which fed their unhappiness. The overzealous scamper for the right vocation occasionally caused chronic depression for students. Fierce classroom competition separated many from their dream professions.

Consequently, alternative academic pursuits fell short of lasting fulfillment. Interest and performance in college studies often diminished. Far too many graduated with baccalaureate and even advanced degrees which left them feeling like empty under-achievers. Unfortunately, all that a significant number accrued was a hefty loan payment coupled with the loss of precious years of searching. Equally unfortunate, turning to Jesus Christ usually did not seem to be a viable option to ease the stress caused by their question.

The Call does not demand that we survey our intellectual acumen personal traits or general skill aptitude. Ephesians 4:1 announces that the children of God are Called to Vocation. God does not expect us to turn to our own devises and scramble to choose a vocation. Our challenge is to trust this fact and struggle with the weighty obligation to live approved as worthy Christians within God's call. The truth is divine purpose does not authorize humanity license to unilaterally seek a vocation. This means that the Christian walk entails being a "prisoner of the Lord", living with complete dependence on Jesus Christ and being freely shackled to divine will.

Bruce reminds the reader they are called to be "members of the new humanity."(2) Bruce further testifies that "members of the Christian society will have in mind not only the society's reputation in the world but the character of [God] who called it into being and the purpose for which [God] so called it." (3)

What do you want to be when you grow up? For Paul "growing up" requires that our lives are a reflection of our high destiny in the Christian ethic. It is ultimately a response to the prophetic witness that the Kingdom of God is at hand working through the will of God; empowered by the Holy Spirit; actively supporting Christian vocation which is securely framed in the teachings of the Lord Jesus. Christians "grow up" in grace to believe they are participating in a beloved community which:

- Is inclusive–including all of God's children regardless of race, gender or socioeconomic status.
- Practices mercy, kindness, and forgiveness in the spirit of scriptures, believing that situations may be settled in peace as opposed to violence, rage and evil confrontation.
- Practices forbearance in response to other's burdens.
- Shares wealth, responsibilities in a setting that espouses equality.

DIVERSITY OF ROLES

According to Young's **Analytical Concordance to the Bible,** "vocation" translates, "a calling". Campbell [4] and Kohler [5] reveal "vocation" is derived from the Latin word **vocare**, which means, "to call".

> Our primary vocation is to be a disciple of Jesus, which means that our professional careers and our personal activities are all subject to the rigors of Jesus' discipline and the power of his promise. Our focus must be on the priority of God's claim on our total life, not just our religious life, because the two cannot meaningfully be separated. From this perspective, there are an almost endless number of jobs in which a Christian can live out his or her vocation. Christian wholeness involves the commitment of one's total life to God, regardless of one's particular work. [6]

> The word 'vocation' has been debased in the modern world by being made synonymous with "occupation"...On the purely secular basis the term 'vocation' is practically meaningless unless God is really there to do the calling, but, on the Christian basis, it is a reasonable word. It still refers, in many cases, to occupation, but the conception is that each occupation can and must be conceived as a ministry. [7]

In his well-known classic, H. Richard Niebuhr conveys four elements that constitute the call to vocation, ministry and service. Cited are:

1) The call to be a Christian described as the call to discipleship of Jesus Christ, to hearing and doing of the Word of God, to repentance and faith, et cetera;
2) The secret call, namely, that inner persuasion or experience whereby a person feels directly summoned or invited by God to take up the work of the ministry;
3) The providential call, which is that invitation and command to assume the work of the ministry which comes through the equipment of a person with the talents necessary for the exercise of the office and through the divine guidance of (their) life by all its circumstances;
4) The ecclesiastical call, that is the summons and invitation extended to (men and women) by some community or institution of the Church to engage in the work of the ministry. (8)

Niebuhr affirms there is a diversity of roles related to the call. He defines, without naming, a variety of known vocations in religious orders, denominations or sacred careers. A chosen few are called to functions as pastor, priest, and ordained minister. Similarly, God calls individuals to cloistered orders, missionary status, higher education and specialized fields requiring academic preparation. Among this group, vocation is validated in religious orders of consecution, ordination, chastity / poverty / obedience, word / sacrament / order or commissions to duties in cited mission fields.

Christian disciples (i.e.; the laity) who assume membership in local congregations are called to a host of functions in that setting. It is possible for you to fulfill your call outside the planned programmatic vision and/

or mission statement of your local congregation. Geographical locations (i.e. Matthew 28:18-20, Acts 1:7,8) may identify the workplace, civic projects, social organizations, volunteer humanitarian ventures or even private random acts of mercy and kindness. One's vocation often starts in their home. The time, place, circumstance and people you engage are God's prerogative.

Vocation must be viewed as an unmerited, divine gift. It is intended to be shared and cultivated as the disciple is led to utilize these in harmonious relationship with their intended recipients in outreach and nurture. Vocation does not call us to divvy up our time into fractured parts (i.e.; career, church, personal space and autonomous adventure). To do so is to create walls which partition us from divine self-revelation.

Perhaps, you can testify that your personally selected vocation restores human dignity, improves human personage and increases the human sense of self-worth. The more important bevy of related questions is does what you do create a binding union with Christ? Have you or do you desire to escape imprisonment which is peculiar to Christian fellowship? Are you securely shackled to the Apostle Paul's exhortation to "walk worthy of the vocation wherewith you are called?" Are you busy doing your own thing? Are your steps ordered and incinct with the Lord's direction?

Depending on your answer, you may be experiencing an unexamined life which is independent of the call. This represents the predicament of being alienated from the Apostle Paul's "a prisoner of the Lord" metaphor. This is an oppositional life, which bypasses the need to be captured and detained in the Savior's love. This is a pride-full life which is ashamed of being bonded forever to the Master's teachings. This is an unfulfilled life, one which forfeits the promise of eternal custody in the New Jerusalem. This is a worldly existence. It resists voluntary servitude to live Christ-centered and Christ-inspired.

What God has prepared for each of us belongs to us alone. You will not be shortchanged. Self-affirmation in selected secular vocations may bankrupt our divine inheritance. Threatened is our call to a holistic life of vocation in Jesus Christ. The battle to secure status, profit, and fulfillment in a meaningful vocation is not ours to fight. The Lord has already won that battle for us. Our purpose in vocation is mutually befriended in a closer walk with Christ. This is a walk of conduct and behavior that connects one harmoniously to a bond of peace. To grow up in this manner is to obtain far more than a profession and job security.

Chapter VII

Called By The Greatest Love

"For God so loved the world, that He gave his only begotten Son, that whosoever believes in him shall not perish, but have everlasting life."

John 3:16, KJV

It is love that asks, that seeks, that knocks, that finds, and that is faithful to what it finds. ***St. Augustine***

CALLED BY GOD

Love has myriad forms and countless, complex faces. It is capable of feeling fickle, which sometimes stumbles into hate; it collides with fantasy and folly, while occasionally seeking unrealistic expectations from targeted individuals. Love engenders a plethora of personal meanings and engulfs innumerable aspects of human expression. Love is essentially humankind's strongest emotional craving, perhaps, more than food, shelter or wealth.

The desire to love is a significant part of human nature. Humans are amiable, gregarious creatures. Paramount for them is the need to participate in meaningful relationships. Yearning to be loved so thoroughly and exclusively in return is a priority sought very early in life. In search of intense affection from a loving source, an infant learns to cry when wet, hungry, lonely, or cold. Instinctively, human life craves tenderness and seeks personal ties. Everyone wants to know they belong to someone. We thrive on being affirmed and authenticated by others' acts of trustworthy love.

The Greek language defines **eros** and **philia** as two descriptions of love, which manifest themselves more specifically in human relationships. The former connotes an esthetic, romantic love that is associated with sexual desire. The latter designates the intimate love between friends and close family members. **Philia**, natural human affection, is expressed with strong feelings of sentiment, in companionship, while endeavoring to protect or share another's well being. Without **eros** and **philia** interacting in the human psyche and emotion, feelings of inadequacy develop. Trust falls into mistrust. Loneliness ensues. Good feelings about one's self do not flourish. Being good to self becomes difficult. Loving self is near impossible.

The theological statement God is love does not constitute a one-way hypothesis which assumes love only derives from God. Love constitutes a three-way communication. Each individual has the responsibility first to love God, "with all their heart, mind and soul," and secondly, "to love their neighbor and finally themselves." (Matthew 22:37-39) Inextricably dependent and interrelated; the God, neighbor and self, relationship cannot exist separately. There can be no fulfillment until we love God first and God alone. **Agape**, the third description of love, calls us to concurrently love all people. All defines neighbor. **Agape** is the love of God which calls us into vocation, ministry and service.

In the midst of this love triangle, we exist in tension. Confusion persists. It is difficult for us to differentiate between **agape** and love expressed as **eros** and **philia**. Divine love does not intend to stimulate a fuzzy visceral feeling or soft, sentimental virtue, nor does it intend to generate an esthetic romance encounter with God. The love of God transcends the secular understanding of intimacy. It is far more than a valued companion. **Agape** is expressed in Christian fellowship: people being touched by God; people being connected to themselves; people touching people in acts of mercy, mission, and ministry.

A LOVING FATHER

The peek-a-boo game is erroneously believed to be wholesome entertainment for a baby. The adult quickly alternates from hiding his face and returning his face. God was here! But, where is God now? Or, where is God anyway? How can I trust the call if I am unable to depend on this God who seems temporary, one who, like the person in the peek-a-boo game appears to be abruptly, in and out of my life?

Young Wiley was visiting his grandparents. As the family gathered for Sunday dinner, grandfather asked his nine-year-old namesake a probing question. "Wiley," grandfather momentarily paused and then carefully proceeded. "What did you like about church today?" This was an E.F. Hutton moment. For when little Wiley spoke, everyone listened. Attention rested on his every word. Then, with a puzzled look and accompanying deep sigh, the seemingly disappointed lad offered an all-telling reply. "The choir sang well. The preacher had everyone saying, Amen! People told me they loved me. They even said, God loves you too, but I did not see God nor Jesus anywhere."

This is normal trust versus mistrust conflict for a child. Many young-in-faith Christian adults share this identical image of God. God's love appears to have peek-a-booed in and out of their constant need for love. Sometimes God seems absent. The result is a trust versus mistrust issue, which prolongs and does not satiate. Like young Wiley, the called children of God expect an in-depth, full-figured image of God in concrete physical dimensions. A speaking, unseen God, who does not appear in Technicolor, Three-Dimension and Dolby sound, fails to be accepted as a trusted agent of **agape** or the Superintendent of a loving relationship.

In **The Captivating Presence**, Albert Edward Day contends; "God is present in reality no matter what unreality our practices and our ponderings imply. [God] is forever trying to establish communication: forever aware of the wrong direction we are taking and wishing to warn us; forever standing at the door of our loneliness."[(2)] Many find difficulty depending on this holy truth. Hence, God's love, which calls disciples, appears to be elusive. God's substance, which rescues with **agape**, is believed to have vacated their grasp.

Remember that vibrant children's hymn, "Jesus Loves Me". The lyrics give the assurance that because little ones are unable to protect themselves, Jesus is ever present to do so. The love of our Savior is described in a trilogy of unquestioned loyalty and announces His authority on earth and in heaven. The Bible says He loves us; He died to prepare a better place for us; Jesus will, one day, escort us to heaven, our eternal home.

As a juvenile, I learned to trust the Christ who was lifted up in that hymn. I never had any reason to challenge this consoling proclamation. During my adolescent years, while dealing with a cathexis with the call, I continuously clung to the simple theological mindset I had come to accept: "Jesus Loves Me." Later, when being down right obstinate to the quiet, lingering cameo appearances of the Holy Spirit, I seldom mistrusted the love of God's presence.

Consequently, the foundation for trusting love develops according to how one enters and completes the first stage of life, trust versus mistrust.[3] I was confident Jesus loved me, perhaps, because I was a warmly touched, lovingly held child. My experience taught me that if you trusted Jesus, the Lord's touch (i.e.; presence, intervention) would be a hedge of protection. So, when I received a hug or a shielding comfort during a threat signal, it was as if Jesus worked through my parents, grandparents, uncles/aunts and others care-takers. I was assured that because Jesus touched all of us, they were given authority to love and touch me.

Furthermore, when a child's primary needs are lovingly met, they ultimately trust that the world around them is good. In believing that "Jesus Loves Me" the child also trusts that good things happen when needs are expressed. What I need must be good; therefore, I am good. God is good too! Our childhood ability to trust Jesus is related to our image of an unseen God, the Father of our Lord.

Such are the implications for a lifelong spiritual readiness for the call. If Jesus loves me, so does His Parent. The spiritually healthy image is of God as a parenting figure, both mother and father. To love God, the Father with unblemished trust is to enter into a relationship which pledges a childlike respect and blind obedience. In return, this loving parent forgives, promises mercy and acts as a protecting, warmly touching parent/guardian to us. [4]

Luke, the physician, in Chapter 15 assures us that God's love resembles a loving father (Luke 15:11-24) and/or loving mother (Luke 15:8-10) who passionately seeks us out. Luke further teaches that this is not an errant God calling from a distance. The God who gives us Jesus in love is not an erratic parent, but gently gathers us in a bond of nurturance.

TRUSTING GOD

The manner in which we trust the love of God expressed through the teachings, ministry and call by Jesus Christ may depend in part on:

- How one experienced love in being touched as a child.
- Whether mother and/or father parented with a loving demeanor or were absent as a delinquent caregiver.
- How hurts were nurtured and disobedience addressed.
- Whether you felt good about yourself because of positive reinforcement.
- Whether caregivers reared you in an environment of hostility and/or insecurity.

The more the above were experienced positively, the chances are that when Called By The Greatest Love, God is answered because God is perceived as being warm and approachable. The initial struggle with the call may be related to how a person's caregivers attended to intimate details of rearing. Depending on the answer, one's rearing either enhanced or hampered basic trust in the call. Such failure or success may have lifelong consequences in the search to recognize that **agape** is associated with answering the call. The ability to respond to the call centers on whether your image of **agape** is remote and wounded or connected and healing.

Make no mistake; **agape** calls us to committed relationship. Does, "till death do us part," threaten our goals for a double life, one with the Greatest Love and the other with secular loves? Why isn't a monogamous relationship with our Creator and Benefactor sufficient? Our mistrusting nature may cause us to consider polygamy, the love of and with an assortment of earthly gods. We qualify our relationship with Jesus by acknowledging our desire to have the best of two worlds. "There is nothing serious between the Savior and me. We are only platonically connected. Plans for a permanent marriage appear to be remote and must remain on hold until wounded desires are healed."

The greatest love is far more than a trusted companion. Divine love is meant to become the inseparable connective tissue, the richly inherited saving fiber which protects the human soul from ever having to perish. Fulton J. Sheen poetically captures the essence of agape's premier expression. "[God's] love would be like the heat of the sun. Those nearest to it would be warm and happy, those who were farthest away would still know its light."(5) What a completely nurturing God! How great a Love! What a loving connection to answer and follow!

Chapter VIII

Called To New Life

"Ye must be born again." *John 3:7(b), KJV*

> "The old order changeth, yielding place to new; And God fulfills [Godself] in many ways, Lest one good custom should corrupt the world." ***Alfred, Lord Tennyson***

YOU MUST BE BORN AGAIN

Curiosity attracts you to the community of faith. Being physically present where Jesus is made evident through signs and wonders seems to be socially correct strategy. After all, it does not hurt, nor does it cost anything. From an emotionally uncommitted distance, you watch miracles improve the lot of others. Vicariously, you feel healed. Still, there is no passion to follow Jesus seriously. The demand for self-surrender and self-denial causes you antagonism.

This is not a rush to judgment, my friend. Your case is closed. Thankfully, Jesus will render a saving verdict. You must be born again! Accept the guaranteed "second chance." Respond to the mandated "must" in a life restored with new identity in Jesus.

Suppose you go to church regularly, but church does not go through you. Your spirit seems unchanged. Reverence is given to Jesus, but it never transfers into any significant intimacy with our Lord and Savior. Perhaps, you live out the Christian faith participating in generous acts of mercy and kindness, and reaching out to people with your time, talent and tithes. Unfortunately, Sunday worship, Bible study and other Christ-centered activities yield only unresolved monotony. There is hope. Privately, seek Jesus. Jesus calls everyone to receive new life. You are next in line to receive it.

The criticizing noise of the crowd with its superficial faith keeps you preoccupied. Embarrassed and/or fearful, you conceal your intense desire to let the Gospel nurture you. Testimonies of true believers who have accepted salvation and reconciliation secretly absorb you. Do not be discouraged. Remove that old restraint which harnesses you. Start over in the enabling power, the Holy Spirit, believing "your destiny will hang on how you hear and answer what Jesus will say." (1)

"You must be born again!" Identify that you have been sought after and singled out. Recognize that you have been called. Isolate yourself from the criticizing crowd. Abandon all superficial curiosity about Jesus. Welcome serious discernment. Then, intensify your new spiritual discovery with acts which demonstrate faith and commitment.

Aspire to be "born of water and the spirit (John 3:5)." Honor your baptism. Wear it with holy enthusiasm. Baptism initiates you into fellowship, and as such, believers enter into a sacred ownership, protected by the love of the triune blessing. Know that your baptism signifies that you have been cleansed and anointed; water washed to advance into a fruitful new creature, cultivated to grow with your call, compelled to faith in your good works.

> To be born again, and to be willing to receive ungrudgingly the gifts that God offers, involves the abandonment of every attempt to become righteous by anything a person may do for themselves, and the willing acceptance of the free gift of grace. Such a complete reorientation is an experience that can well be likened to physical birth, for it is an emergence from darkness into light, when the restricted and confined is at last set free. (2)

When you are born again, an open, visible relationship with Jesus commences. The peripheral, physical posture among the criticizing crowd loses appeal. This is replaced by an inward surrender to faith away from human stumbling blocks. Not only does the born-again person live to reflect the Gospel, he/she also embraces the opportunity to confess Jesus Christ outwardly.

Nicodemus carried a reserved reverence for the "teacher come from God (John 3:2)." A superficial beginning of faith swelled within him.

The Pharisee obtained the news that Jesus cleansed the Temple (John 2:13-22) and, during the height of Passover (John 2:23) performed miracles. "Are these truly the prophesized signs and wonders of things to come", proposed Nicodemus. A hidden desire to converse with this unorthodoxed Rabbi lingered in Nicodemus. Still, quietly, he congregated among his curious, oppositional colleagues.

Confusion and uncertainty haunted him. Nicodemus craved clarification. He yearned for more than casual observation of Jesus from a detached, confrontative vantage point. A meaningful meeting with this "learned teacher" seemed to be the solution. Cognizant of his vacancy, the "ruler of the Jews" visited Jesus under the cloak of darkness (John 3:2).

Why darkness? Was Nicodemus fearful or ashamed? Being seen interacting with Jesus amounted to certain professional career suicide. Did Nicodemus regard Jesus as a peer or inferior to him? After all, this "teacher comes from God" functioned as an independent itinerant, not associated with mainstream Jewish religion.

Kruse emphases that "night appears to have negative connotations. In John 9:4, Jesus urges people to work in the day, for the night is coming when no one can work. In John 11:10, Jesus says that "those who walk in the night stumble because they have no light."[3]

Edwards cites several who questioned Nicodemus' choice of night for his visitation to meet Jesus:

> Augustine thinks his timidity a symptom of carnal-mindedness (Homily 11.5); Calvin sees an example of 'frail and transient faith', while Luther cites his obtuseness as a proof that only those who are called are able to believe (Rupp and Watson 1969: 322). Eriugena thinks him a

> specimen of faith perfected but not enriched by works (p. 314 Migne). [4]

None-the-less, though ignorant of the sovereign power Jesus possessed over him, Nicodemus doubtfully and awkwardly, went to Jesus.

Without hesitation, Jesus emphatically called Nicodemus to new life. The expectation is not to regress literally to the fetal stage of development. What being born again mandates is a conversion from his present posture dominated by piety, position and privilege. His earth-bound habits which were rooted in rigorous religious practice excluded the Lord Jesus. A spiritual metamorphosis is necessary. The former Nicodemus must receive Jesus as a new person.

> ...Jesus has used a basic earthly category – human birth – to illuminate a profound spiritual reality...Born again! The phrase is arresting and fresh, alive with meaning. Another chance, starting over, new life! Is it possible? That is exactly what Jesus is saying. [5]

Jesus' striking admonishment created several problems for Nicodemus. The statement cut across the grain of the Torah. It shook the foundation of all he learned and taught. For him, the Torah contained the divine truth which was not subject to any new contingencies. These scriptures contained the guidelines for Jewish life. The Torah represented his primary source for faith and hope.

Jewish Scripture revealed that entrance into the Kingdom of God constituted an inherited birth rite upon resurrection of the dead at the end of time. Only denial of faith in God and/or any defection from the Law of Moses forfeited that holy promise. Nicodemus dismissed the idea that the Kingdom of God described an earthly social reality or a God connection to human faith.

Imagine this distinguished Pharisee being humbled by the admonishment of a rustic stranger. Sanhedrin ruling council members were not accustomed to such deep-seated challenge around matters of Jewish law and theological interpretation. Jesus shattered his stance on traditional beliefs. So intrusive was Jesus, that Nicodemus, an industrious religious leader, now felt mediocre and like a failure. His hands were full, holding on to old valued Jewish teachings, while wrestling with the newly discovered truths of Jesus.

Jesus reminded Nicodemus of the Old Testament story of "God Judges with the Serpent (Numbers 21:4-9)" and Moses' "Lifting Up the Brazen Serpent". Then, from the perspective of New Testament teaching, John 3:16 (i.e.; believing in the Son / receive eternal life), new interpretation of the Kingdom of God clouded his current foundation. Spiritual poverty raised its wounded head in Nicodemus. Yet, Jesus sought Nicodemus and singled him out.

Soon, Nicodemus would come of age, boldly choosing Jesus as his first and only love. Jesus never intended to deny the truths of the Torah. The purpose was to introduce new life with the Gospel which fulfilled the Old Testament prophecy.

The Pharisee would proclaim Jesus as the very substance of God, who embodied the identical living Word (i.e.; the Son of God). When we return to Nicodemus and witness the fruits of his new life – the unleashing of God's grace to form a new creature – we will observe the radical change in a confused and uncertain human life. Jesus announces this particular "must" emphatically to everyone.

CALLED TO WITNESS

> On my way to school one morning in early spring, I stopped to listen to the song of a mockingbird perched upon the topmost twig of the tallest tree in the woods. He had heard, I take it, the drum-beat of Springtime. The dirge of the winter had changed to the Te Deum of May. The sun had pointed his finger of fire at the ice and snow until they had cried themselves into running streams. The field had thrown their winter cloaks back and exposed their bosoms of daisies and buttercups. The woods whispered softly the joy of coming summer. Filled with these rare bits of the heavenly, the glad mocking bird, with throat distended, wings plumed, and eyes upon the sun, sent forth notes that were almost divine. Darts of ecstasy lifted him now and again, from the twig upon which he stood, and tumbling over and over in that sweet springtime glory, he gained his position without a break in his song.(6)

Charles Albert Tindley vividly captured the joy of being born again.(7) He introduced an excited mockingbird. It was called to witness the harmony of the changing seasons, from the dormant winter to the joy experienced during the great expectations of spring. The corresponding seasons may express the reality of the ever-changing climate of the Christian journey. The mockingbird is made privy to the new possibilities, where old operations cease to have further value and purpose. Along with our feathered friend, we watch the blossoming of God's abundant grace. Like Nicodemus, we must learn to endure our empty winters if we are to be born again with the breaking of "spring".

Witness the thankful rejoicing. During the long, chilly darkness, the spirited roots burrow into the hardened soil. Slowly, at first invisibly, new roots turn outward. Finally, the new dawn of spring arrives. Earth is poised to be "born again". In response, the praising mockingbird serenades the dormant life with a cheerful hallelujah. The cold, static life with its restless hibernation, surrenders to a warm, free flowing, newly enlighten energy. This is the time. The barren existence has been replenished.

Be advised. While quiet and isolated, winter is not an unproductive time. God gives these dormant, long chilling, and dark nights for us to burn the midnight oil. It is an active, solitary time to listen and learn about God's secret call. The wintry journey is God's gift to us so we can reflect on the circumstances; collect errant thoughts and prepare for new possibilities. Sometimes this rest and renewal period is mentally, emotionally and spiritually painful. At other points, it is uplifting and unbinding. Then, there are the inactive, private retreats when all is silent and serene. Nicodemus retreated to such an existence often after visiting Jesus in the darkness of the chilling night.

New life parallels the classic metamorphosis of the encapsulated caterpillar. Wanting to become a butterfly, the underdeveloped creature works to free itself. It patiently awaits the freeing moment, when finally, the new creature breaks the isolating cocoon. Tindley brings alive for our disclosure, the soul yet born of the Spirit. Spring denotes a spiritual metamorphosis when the soul is changed, finally free to liberate itself and others. Spring releases an explosive grace for a withered faith. Spring illuminates uncharted direction for a new life's journey.

The chilling isolation was well spent by Nicodemus. He abandoned the common interferences which make discernment difficult. With resolute character, Nicodemus conquered this icy human existence and was released from the frozen cocoon-like isolation of confusion and uncertainty about Jesus. New life made clear the obligation to believe in the living God as a parenting figure. "Whosoever shall not receive the Kingdom of God as a little child shall not enter therein (Mark 10:15)." In turn, a humble babe in Jesus named Nicodemus emerged into his spring assured of eternal protection.

Evidence collaborates that Nicodemus was born again. While still an active Pharisee and member of the Sanhedrin, Nicodemus intensified his faith by: 1) believing that Jesus was truly the Son of God; 2) believing that because Jesus became flesh, Jesus was subject to human death, and; 3) believing that unlike Moses' lifting up the brass serpent to spare the penalty of death for the rebellious Israelis, Jesus would be lifted up to pay for all human with the penalty of death.

Nicodemus spiritually left the curious, critical ranks of his colleagues. Also, his work demonstrated an intensified relationship with Jesus:

- In John 7:50-52, he speaks on behalf of Jesus before the Sanhedrin, which is confused over Christ. The court is ready to condemn Jesus without the opportunity to explain His actions.
- In John19:38-42, with the assistance of Joseph of Arimathea, they claim the corpse of Jesus for burial. It is Nicodemus who purchases the expenses species for the important ritual of embalming.

When Nicodemus, you or I experience being born again, our lives will never be perfect. We must be continuously fortified with visits to Jesus in privacy. Sometimes, we return under the cloak of secrecy and darkness. Jesus is never finished with us. The excited mockingbird depends on the yearly collapse of winter into spring. Even in a dedicated life which is committed to a lasting relationship with Jesus, there is always the need to revive new life.

Edwards stresses a constant truth taught by John Wesley. "New birth consists not of having been once baptized, but in continuing evidence of faith, hope and love." [8] Wesley analizes these three marks of the New Birth citing "Faith is a disposition wrought by God in the heart. Hope is called full assurance. Love springs to our neighbors from God and is manifest in outward works, but not mere outward service. Wesley's application of the marks hinge on several pertinent questions. Are you born of God? Not what were you made in baptism, but what are you now?" [10]

The journey to attain new life is like a roller coaster ride; the up and down cycles compromise a sustained faith. We vacillate between carefully ordering our Christian walk and stumbling over our superficial faith, short-sighted hope and self-serving love. Being born again requires constant spiritual discipline even with the changing speeds and altitudes of our daily existence. The only misfortune is to achieve new life and believe that one effort (i.e.; of identifying, isolating and intensifying) is sufficient to sustain the life long journey. New life must be sustained during our challenging winters when the mockingbird in us has only a solemn dirge to sing.

Chapter IX

Called To Unity

"There is one body, and one Spirit, even as ye are called in one hope of calling."

Ephesians 4:4, KJV

"The real unity of the church must not be organized, but exercised." ***Johannes Lilje***

SACRED SPACE

For a moment, visualize your church sanctuary. Hues of color, degrees of sound volume, selected signage/symbols (i.e.; cross, stained glass windows, flags, banners, candles) reflect your congregation's understanding of the ever-present Godhead. The furnishings (i.e.; altar, pulpit, lectern, pews) all have both practical purposes and liturgical meaning. Air, light, and temperature convene in this three-dimensional sanctuary to assist hearing, seeing, and feeling the Gospel of Jesus Christ. Here, followers of Jesus Christ gather, not only to worship, but also for community sharing of traditions, culture, mores, and for supporting the assembly of disciples.

The architectural design expresses a theology of space, the assumed nature of God's height, width and depth of communication. As a result of prayerful thought, prudent use of earthbound dimension, your sacred space gives glory, honor, and praise to the universal call. It functions as a legitimate habitat for extensive individual and corporate spiritual formation. Your church sanctuary is truly a significant extremity within the larger Body of Christ.

A JOURNEY WITH MANY DIFFERENT FACES

Now, look into the many faces you fellowship with in your local congregation. None is a carbon copy of another. They are diverse in age, socioeconomic status, personality, perhaps ethnicity or within the same ethnicity are dissimilar because of different socio-geographic origin. While they profess the same denomination, quite possibly, a variety of religious beliefs confront established doctrine and polity. Different values and theological stances may promote widespread religious thought. Personal life experiences correspond with an array of biblical interpretations. Oddly enough, your congregation is Called To Unity. It bonds together, having "one spirit, even as ye are called in one hope of your calling; one Lord, one faith, one baptism, one God and Father of all." (Ephesians 4:4-6)

Initially, the Church at Ephesus was intended recipient of this cited text. The Letter's message was as important to that congregation in 62 A.D. as to your congregation today. A major focus addressed the responsibility of Christian disciples to practice unity within the membership. The epistle writer emphasized that unity for the Church defined a citizenship for all believers. All are fellow citizens in unity with God, walking together with the Holy Spirit.

Jews and Gentiles comprised the bulk of believers at Ephesus. The former were the descendants of the Israelites who relocated in Asia Minor after the Babylonian exile. As Jewish Christians, many continued the religious traditions of their ancient heritage. For these Jews, Gentiles, while accepted as Christian converts saved through Jesus Christ, were still considered strangers to the Hebrew God's covenant. They were regarded as pagans because many did not refrain from the practice of idolatry.

To compound the issue of unity, the Church at Ephesus encountered diversity concerns. The fellowship was male and female. Members reflected the range of the socio-economic strata. It included free citizens, indentured servants and slaves. Because the Triune God was worshipped along with a bevy of other gods, the community resembled a polytheistic cult. The epistle writer called the entire Church at Ephesus to accept the Body of Christ as the end of all cults. The goal entailed pledging to grow together in the freedom of Christ. Allegiance was expected to Christ only. This schism created a dividing wall among the Christians at Ephesus. Unity was essential. The invis ible wall which harbored discord had to be destroyed in spite of the fac

hat Christ and the Church were viewed through the lenses of multi-
:ultural traditions.

NO DIVISION OR CONFRONTATION

Vith fascination, I watch the hundreds of geese that invade the Marshall
'ones farm across Shiloh Road from our home in Westtown Township,
Vest Chester, Pennsylvania. Unlike your congregation, they are a carbon
:opy of one another. The geese have inherited near identical size, body
ypes, feather structure and color. Their gaits, quacking sounds, eating
ıabits and flying dynamics do not deviate much. Subsequently, their
ıabitual traits and innate purpose in God's created order appears to be
n unity. Geese always seem to be growing together, depending on the
lock with instinctive allegiance. Foremost, no geese is ever a stranger
o the flock. All are fellow geese bonded in a common determination.
'ogether, like your church membership, they are unified in their forma-
ion and expression.

They teach humanity what being Called to Unity should inspire a
:ongregation to achieve. Annually, they migrate. During late September,
he geese begin to congregate in a habitual behavior of corporate unity.
watch them glide through the sky in intricate formations. They travel
s one body, over our property, which seems to be one of several aerial
ighways divinely designed for them. Each of the geese assumes its'
lace in the formation. Whether leading the flock, navigating on either
he right or left flank or bringing up the rear, there is contentment in
heir assigned task. No position appears greater than another. All geese
eem to delegate themselves to a subordinate role, functioning to inspire
armony during the aerial mission. Together, they typify the meaning of
ommunity and Shalom. There is no "I" in their team.

The web-footed species soar gracefully in their God-given aerodynamic formations. Their unified wing flapping reduces the resistance of the air. Such strategy enhances greater mobility as they travel. Together, committed to their own function within the flock, they collectively decrease the load for the body. I am always astonished by the intricate teamwork and brilliant strategy which the geese constantly display.

When one goose tires during flight, the other geese immediately regroup and modify the formation to decrease the drag. If for any reason one falls to the earth, another follows like an EMT specialist. Like the Good Samaritan, there is a commitment to be their neighbor's keeper.

The continuous quacking is not idle noise. These are signals for purposeful communication during flight. Perhaps, they are encouraging each other to remain united during the journey. As they quack, the geese renew a basic trust in their mission. This behavior parallels the moments when congregations gloriously offer to God, in praise and thanksgiving the uplifting hymns of the Church.

In their involuntary behavior, the geese mirror the message in I Corinthians 12:4-6. As the geese are essentially carbon copy look-alikes, they are task specific. In this respect, they look like your congregation. Observe how effectively individual differences respond to unity. Again, geese bring their individual gifts to facilitate the well being of the flock's indivisible flight formation. There is no division or confrontational wall which separates any goose for any reason.

Together, they fly in a bonding mode, "all-for-one and one-for-all." Together, the geese are naturally imbued with one hope through their quacking signals. They glide as one body, a created species of God with one spirit, called instinctively together in one hope of destination and purpose. Alone or fragmented, they are reduced to being nothing but unfulfilled, aimless birds. Without unity, the geese are dimin ished to helpless survivors struggling in the company of look-alike feathered strangers.

A COMMON SACRED GOAL

Your divinely purpose-driven congregants are not always evenly yoked by theological conformity. However, participants wrap themselves around a primary goal. What God's called children share is their common bond. The members of local congregations join in a mission to serve Christ, the Church and the community because they believe they are Called To Unity.

So, believers collectively search for answers. They accept the promise that Jesus Christ's' self-involvement guides them to Go! Baptize! Teach! (Matthew 28:18-20)

Jesus Christ calls members into a sacred fellowship to reach those who are hurt, humiliated and hungry. Together, they are expected to fully ascribe to the mandate of unity in the ministry of mercy and kindness. Together, congregants are called to gather with one heart: one in the identical spirit walk, functioning to spread the Kingdom of God. To exist, "alive in Christ", is to serve all-for-one, one-for-all, all serving one Christ harmoniously for the preservation of the Body.

When one answers the call to this holy union, his/her should become aware of his/her sacred location in Christ. Together, the called community is prompted to draw upon its guaranteed spiritual inheritance. All hopes prevail in Jesus Christ as Lord and Savior. All hope is immersed in the truth of the Gospel. Followers of Christ believe this hope holds the saving message. Believer's rest in a hope identified as eternal life.

It is because of their individual and collective experiences that the members of your congregation have an unrivaled story to tell. Their lives preach like sermons with appropriate text and topic, like the people depicted in the Holy Scriptures. Your worshipping community may resonate with the lot of Israel. From time to time, the ups and downs of Paul's Christian communities describe your congregation's circumstances.

You have doubters like Thomas. A few carry the pious indignation of the Pharisees. Big egos occasionally dominate church administration. Although not perfect, these are the called children of a perfect sovereign God. Be comforted in the fact that God knows why every member is present in your congregation. With continued faith, in a spirit of unity, you and your congregation will grow together.

Since the Day of Pentecost, the Holy Spirit has operated in the Church of every generation. God has collectively called the members of local congregations, small mission-minded groups, including nations. Christian movements, faith-based initiatives, social justice emphases and worship revivals are evidences of the Holy Spirit working among the many calls within groups of people.

Focus on the selected few that God has set aside to answer the call to ordained ministry. Up close, you have witnessed how the called ascend from the pew to the pulpit. Perhaps, their testimony personally persuaded you to contemplate the secret, inward call that led you to accept your profession of faith. You shared a significant part of their call journey. You participated in their call. In this unifying community of faith, someone is always placed before you to challenge you to hear the voice of God. Their experiences motivated others in the cause to serve Christ. These set-apart disciples act as important role models, mentors, and tutors during a host of teachable moments to many who witnessed their call in actions.

These Christians have heard the call, answered obediently and are willing to follow Christ. No longer is diversity a burdensome, disconnected entity. Your congregation is on the cutting-edge to spread the Gospel and share the faith of the Body of Christ. Together, members bring their individual gifts and graces. Together, like the geese that congregate on the Marshall Jones Farm, God's children are Called to Unity in a bond to function all-for-one and one-for-all.

Chapter X

Go! Baptize! Teach!

And Jesus came and spoke unto them saying, "All power is given unto me in heaven and in earth. Go ye therefore, and teach all nations, baptizing them in the name of the Father, and of the Son, and of the Holy Ghost: Teaching them to observe all things whatsoever I have commanded you and, lo, I am with you always, even unto the end of the world.

Matthew 28:18-20, KJV

A church exist for the double purpose of gathering in and sending out. Anonymous

CALLED TO EVANGELIZE NEW CHRISTIANS

Early in the 1990's, the Eastern Pennsylvania Conference of the United Methodist Church unfolded a strategic plan. The goal was to transform local congregations by empowering them to be in serious mission. The vision encouraged local congregations to advocate a spiritual movement intended to recover our Wesleyan evangelistic heritage as established in the Great Commission by:

- Calling people to new life in Jesus Christ,
- Nurturing people to be disciples of Jesus Christ in God's community,
- Addressing the needs in each community where our congregations are located.[1]

The people of faith were encouraged to discern prayerfully about their primary purpose for gathering. The need existed to restore local church identity to being doers of the Word: to Go! Baptize! Teach! This was a call for an action-oriented Christian movement. Many local churches envisioned a fresh appreciation for change in their attitude and behavior as servants for people in their communities.

During the period of July 1996 – April 2000, I served an inner city urban church, which responded to congregational transformation. From the beginning of this congregation's service to God, it committed itself to the welfare of the community. This local church reflected its mission statement and was identified with a host of outreach and onsite ministries. Emmanuel United Methodist Church had a heart to improve the lot of the surrounding community.

Most of the congregants walked to church. They lived in the neighborhood. They were family and friends who interacted with the people, institutions and circumstances of that location. Allow me to share the article I wrote. It demonstrates how the impact of the evangelical movement in the Eastern Pennsylvania Conference's Strategic Plan, miraculously, transformed the Emmanuel Church Parsonage. [2] This is a story of a local congregation which believed they were called to Go! Baptize! Teach!

Adjacent this North Philadelphia community-based church stands its parsonage. This charming three-story brownstone is an architectural gem designed for comfortable urban living during the early 1900's. High ceilings and spacious rooms have been the hallmark of this building's elegant splendor.

Oddly enough, the parsonage was usually vacant for several decades. Renting the parsonage proved to be near fatal. Selling it was not an option because fair market value was impossible to obtain. Deep in Emmanuel's soul was the gnawing conviction that the parsonage was intended to be mission space in the spreading of Christ's Kingdom. The congregation believed God would resurrect this space in time. Emmanuel never wavered in this faith. This local church:

- Persisted in prayerful discussion and faithful planning about the valuable ideal space,
- Maintained a self-identification that was consistent with the needs, interest and lot of the community, and,
- Waited on the Lord in good courage for new direction.

PHOENIX II

In 1995, something happened! It was an idea whose time had come. Emmanuel had endured. Finally, God had intervened to feed both community and church with the nourishment of grace. On that appointed day, Mr. Melvin Harrison met with the Trustee Board, and then pastor, Rev. Varlyna D. Wright. Mr. Harrison had a plan. He was seeking a shared ministry with a community-minded church to rehabilitate drug abusers in a neighborhood residential program.

Melvin came with personal and professional experience. He is a recovered drug abuser, having completed the, "One Day at a Time", program. Mr. Harrison also, has earned credentials in drug counseling and management. Today, the Emmanuel parsonage thrives in a new mission. It has been reconstructed for dormitory living. Phoenix II, most appropriately named, houses up to 30 male clients. Mr. Harrison functions as the President and CEO.

The name Phoenix is reference to a mythical Egyptian bird that rose renewed from its own ashes after 50 years of being consumed by fire. Phoenix II is a non-profit organization in which drug abusers are assigned to the facility for 90-day periods. The clients receive treatment, drug education, medical care, counseling, job placement and training, and new coping skills that are socially acceptable.

The courts remands selected clients for placement. Others are referred from as far away as the Baltimore, Maryland Department of Human Services. Approximately 260 people have graduated since its inception. Many have returned home as fathers, husbands, and gainfully employed as professionals and skilled tradesmen.

Spiritual enrichment is at the heart of the Phoenix II rehabilitation goal. Clients are a vital part of Emmanuel's worship experience. The Phoenix II Recovery Gospel Choir is no stranger to revivals and Sunday worship at Emmanuel.

Twice a day, group counseling occurs in Emmanuel's fellowship hall. Group counseling is mandatory for residents, but any male or female drug abusers may attend. Clients assist the Trustee Board in maintenance and general upkeep of the property. The Pastor-Parish Relations Committee has allocated a part-time janitor's position to a client who is in the program. Recently, the United Methodist Men of the Emmanuel congregation launched its quarterly prayer breakfast with Phoenix II for a time of Christian fellowship.

The congregation supports workshops, seminars and festive occasions sponsored by Phoenix II. The role of the pastor has been well received. The pastor provides individual and family counseling. He also provides information about re-entrance into society after rehabilitation. Other members come for baptism instruction and planning for weddings. Some participate in the weekly Bible studies. Recently, the current pastor started a weekly group workshop which discusses topics such as spirituality (getting high on Christ), healthy living and eating habits, anger management, returning to the community, and cultural diversity.

The Phoenix II story reveals just one nuance out of which congregational transformation may evolve. It imparts that sometimes-creative models of ministry may be the brainchild of the Holy Spirit. We witness with all our planning that we must allow the Holy Spirit to broaden our goals of mission and service.

What may a congregation learn from this transforming miracle? Our risen Lord Jesus Christ is calling congregations to:

- Be inclusive and open-minded during prayer and planning. You do not know who God is calling the congregation to touch.
- Connect with said community needs and interest. Disregard your unilateral thought.
- Pay attention to the people of your locale. What do you know about them?
- Accept them as they are. Evangelism begins with reaching out and in to God's children where and how they are.
- Invite them to become a part of your fellowship, as you were called by **agape**.

CONGREGATIONAL MISSION

The mission of each congregation should be to make the Godhead visible and audible through their earnest actions. Therefore, the local congregation is called and equipped to be the physically, close-up, outreaching extremity of Christ in the community. This mission offers tangible opportunities for others to grow closer to Christ. Called congregations are the primary hands available to work in God's vineyards.

When the vision was realized, the Phoenix II staff, along with the Emmanuel congregation reflected on the apparent reasons for this miracle:

- Well-intended Council on Ministries is paramount.
- Sensitive models for ministry must be authentically people-oriented.
- A Christ-centered vision is necessary if the goals are expected to transform others in need.
- Prayer and corporate worship must reflect the specific mission.

When Jesus says, "Go! Baptize! Teach!", Jesus is in the forefront blazing the path for us. The Holy Spirit is like a headlight pointing and directing us to the real and felt needs of others. Throughout this Emmanuel parsonage transformation experience, the congregation, Mr. Harrison, Pastor Wright and I were to faithfully pondered: What will our prayers facilitate next? How will the Holy Spirit complete this mission?

God's gracious plan for the scores of Phoenix II consumers was constantly unfolding. While we started with the mission at very different times, an omni-present Caller tied and linked our gifts and graces together. It was as if our interventions constituted the work of a family of God. The purposefully scheduled timing of our separate call journeys connected at 17th and York Streets in the heart of an awesome North Philadelphia vision, Phoenix II, for ministry and service. We were all called and chosen to be the "them" in Matthew 28:16-20 who acted in Jesus' name. Together, the three of us were intended to be the disciples summoned to "Go! Baptize! Teach!" the Phoenix II flock, along with Emmanuel United Methodist Church congregation.

Chapter XI

Spiritual Gifts for Spirit-filled Calls

"Now there are diversities of gifts, but the same Spirit. And there are differences in administration, but the same Lord. And there are diversities of operation, but it is the same God which worketh all in all."

I Corinthians 12:4-6, KJV

The existence of a gift is a call to exercise it. Eyes are purposeless unless they exercise the function of sight...disuse of a limb results in paralysis or atrophy, so doctors order patients up soon after surgery. Similarly, exercise is the only way to prevent a gift's lapse or collapse. If you don't use it, you lose it. (In Leslie B. Flynn. 19 Gifts of the Spirit, pp 220-221).

PURPOSE OF SPECIAL SPIRITUAL GIFTS

There is an abundant variety of spiritual gifts, which are purposely distributed to assist Christian believers act on their call. Morris reveals that those in especially close touch with the divine have special spiritual gifts which imbue them with a particular "enthusiasm" for their call.(1) Flynn prefers the term "charisma" and adds "a spiritual gift confers a unique anointing qualification with is granted by the Holy Spirit."(2) Every believer receives the Holy Spirit which empowers them as they approach their appointed task. Turner, in a discussion to convey the Apostle Paul's understanding of spiritual gifts, explains the term "charisma" is a concrete expression of grace expressed in a Trinitarian disclosure.(3)

The Apostle Paul identifies and defines spiritual gifts in several Epistles of the New Testament. He categorizes these as follows:

1) gifts of utterance – prophecy, evangelism, teaching, the pasturing order, exhortation and shepherding;
2) gifts of serving others – supporting roles, hospitality, giving, mercy of kindness, faith and discernment;
3) gifts of miracles and healing; and
4) gifts of insight, wisdom and knowledge.

Spiritual gifts are conferred to accomplish only God's purpose. Clearly, these gifts are in the sole possession of the Holy Spirit. Oftentimes, they are a "one event" gift residing in a once chosen called recipient. They should never be utilized as license for self-aggrandizement. Also, human intervention cannot give spiritual gifts altered purpose, broader efficiency or additional proficiency. Recipients cannot improve spiritual gifts. These charismatic endowments exist only for the sacred advantage and edification of the Church. Through selective human participation, these manifestations of the Spirit express the creative intention of God in and among called disciples.

"The purpose of spiritual gifts is to enable each member of the body to serve, love and encourage others, thus making a 'constructive', 'edifying' contribution to the upbuilding of the church. Just as Jesus set before himself the goal of edifying (building) his church (Matthew 16:18), so Paul saw his task to be the edification (not the tearing down) of the church (1 Cor 3:9; 2 Cor 10:8; 12:19; 13:10), and the Corinthians are urged, "Let all things be done for edification." (1 Cor 14:26) [4]

Biblical accounts reveal individuals called to perform awesome wonders utilizing spiritual gifts. Cited are events which demand herculean effects and tedious campaigns requiring phenomenal accomplishment. God does not merely call, give instructions and terminate the communication, nor, do we obediently respond only to discover essential direction and guidance has not been provided. Spiritual gifts are incapable of deception. Charisma will not abandon calls.

SPIRITUAL GIFTS VS. TALENTS

Do not confuse spiritual gifts with talents. Similarity relates them. Matthew reveals talents are also derived from a freely-giving Christ. The gospel recorder further recommends we accept our talents as thrifty and appreciative stewards. In the Parable of the Talents (Matthew 25:14-30), Jesus teaches that every talent, must be recognized as valued by the Giver. Oh! Yes, if you do not use your talents, you may lose them. Our responsibility is to discharge these talents in a faithfully prudent manner. Talents flourish with constant practice and frequent exercise.

A major difference exists between spiritual gifts and talents. The latter may render themselves beneficial for Christian service. However, talents may afford the owner fame, fortune and/or self-satisfaction.

Consider the honed talents of artists, chefs, musicians, athletes, or the chess player. Human beings are generally incapable of applying their talents consistently at high levels. These gifts may deteriorate with increased chronological ages or diminish because of progressive disinterest. Talents can fail during dubious performance. Spiritual gifts are God's remedy for human failure. In them, a distinctive qualifying possession of divine favor out distances human talents.

Talents are generally the result of natural, creative ability. Their administration and operation occur in the unfolding of personal hereditary traits, our innate aptitude and/or acquired skill. Their successful maturity is the result of a sustained learning curve experience. Recipients sharpen their talents with mental, physical or social fitness in an enhancing performance environment. Human beings need talents. They are essential gifts for survival and adaptation to environmental challenges.

Flynn concurs, "Non-Christians possess talent through common grace…these are not spiritual gifts. Only believers are gifted spiritually. Talents have to do with techniques and methods. Gifts are spiritual abilities. Talents result out of natural, innate power. Gifts represent spiritual endowment." [5] I tend to take the position that, in some instances, talents are spiritual gifts in disguise, waiting for the recipient to use them exclusively in the work of Jesus Christ. When talents revert to spiritual gifts status, perhaps they are enthusiasm and charisma whose time has come to grace one's call.

Tabitha (Acts 9:36-43) was blessed with specific natural, creative ability. God endowed this woman with dexterous hands combined with tremendous fine motor skill in her fingers. Her inherited hand-eye coordination facilitated a keen faculty for artistic crafting. These talents served Tabitha well. She was known to be proficient in needlework and sewing.

Making coats, garments, and other inner wearing apparel consumed her time. Joppa, the main port of Judea, resting along the Mediterranean Sea coast, appeared to be the perfect place to erect a flourishing garment industry. With all the imported fabric available, the sky was the limit for fame and fortune. Talent and location - what a perfect match to launch a successful business career.

Tabitha declined. This disciple understood her calling and envisioned a sacred vocation. She had no ambition to hone God's talent for fame, fortune, or self-satisfaction. Her talents were a gift used to honor God in social service and human advocacy. The one named Gazelle, perhaps for her antelope-like swiftness, chose to promote her talents for a spirit-filled call. Tabitha cultivated her talent. I believe divine inspiration transformed her talent as a spiritual gift. Christ and destitute people were her only concern. As an appreciative steward, Tabitha dared to believe all she possessed belonged to God.

Tabitha was a faithful disciple whose spiritual gift "clothed the naked" (Matthew 25:36). She elected to respond to Christ's message of being her neighbor's keeper. The epitome of Christian charity, Tabitha concentrated on using her gifts to serve the marginalized widows and orphans of Joppa. These were the left out, abandoned, citizens of Joppa, living on the fringes of society, the lowly and forgotten. Tabitha not only made them clothing, but she also gave hope to these economically vulnerable children of God. Her loving kindness was the sign of Christ dwelling among them. In Tabitha, the promise of shalom was exposed for all to see. The Holy Spirit used her talent as a segue for a major call to evangelism in Joppa. Hers were the spiritual gifts of utterance and serving others.

Sadly, Tabitha dies as swiftly as her nickname, Gazelle, implies. The widows openly grieve. They were not able to accept her death. Tabitha's life-giving charity could not be replaced. More importantly, she was their living model of the Christian gospel. A pillar of the community of faith was taken abruptly.

GOD USES ORDINARY PEOPLE

It has been established that God calls ordinary people-sometimes chronic failures-to extra ordinary acts of charisma or awesome wonders. Surprisingly, a familiar disciple is poised to dispense his unrevealed spiritual gift to reverse Tabitha's untimely demise. For such a time as this, we witness how the spiritual gifts of miracles imbued a chosen person to holiness in divine service. Peter was called with spiritual gifts to resurrect Tabitha from death.

Peter was a leader in the Joppa Christian community. His faith and practice reached far beyond our recollection of him immediately before Jesus' death. It is refreshing to know our transgressions are forgotten and the Holy Spirit's transcendent power is able to deliver us to our potential. Imagine the Peter we remember in the Gospel being imbued with charisma, the spiritual gift to influence death from having the final word. Peter fell on his knees in prayer. Resurrection power was not in Peter's personal possession. It belonged to the risen Lord who defied death for everyone on Calvary.

It is not Peter who performs the miracle. However, Peter utilizes the conferred spiritual gift which summons the Lord Jesus Christ and testifies that Tabitha's death had created a crisis in the Joppa community. Even with such an awesome spirited gift, Peter was at Jesus' mercy. With Tabetha's resurrection, God's compassionate love (**agape**) was made visible.

Spiritual gifts enhance our potential for a Christ-centered persona. Many times, they are only a "one event" gift to a once chosen called recipient. Spiritual gifts can never die. They are in the possession of a living Comforter and Savior.

SPIRITUAL GIFTS IN ACTION

Methodist Home For Children in Philadelphia, Pennsylvania has always been graced with staff who saw their employment as a call to vocation, ministry and/or service. Their living testimonies give credence to the fact that it is possible to utilize spiritual gifts in the workplace. Methodist's well-documented archives suggest that, through 126 years of continuous service, many staff, board members, local churches and volunteers have been empowered with special authentic qualification to serve this faith-based agency. Good stewards with a variety of spiritual gifts have been a blessing to children, families, and individuals served.

I possess an eternal portrait of the video showing Irene Freeman playing with her "Suga-Buggas" (the beloved name of children in her pre-school classroom). Irene was imbued with holy enthusiasm and charisma. Her spiritual gifts not only edified the church she attended, but these holy endowments also directed her to serve, love, and encourage the little souls she touched daily at Methodist. Ms. Freeman gave the best of her ability for the common good of the Educare Learning Center. Furthermore, nothing interfered with her commitment to vocal give praise and offer thanksgiving while she worked. Irene also touched the lives of parents and staff as she ministered with the spiritual gift of helps (i.e.; assistance, lending a hand).

At Irene's Memorial Service, all in attendance heard her "final words" on that heart-moving video clip which was produced before her illness. As her Suga-Buggas played, she acknowledged her spiritual gift, by dramatically stating, "this is what I do for a living." Irene Freeman was not elected to be physically resurrected immediately after death and returned to earthly life as Tabitha. None-the-less, she completed her earthly call journey to service with dignity. We claim that God replied, "Well done my good and faithful servant." She was a witness and believer, even in her employment. So, Irene's work was not in vain. The manner in which she answered her call guaranteed her resurrection when Jesus returns and ushers her into everlasting life. And, because she lives with the living God, Irene's spiritual gifts continue to be alive and distributed among us here at Methodist today. Irene's story demonstrates that all spiritual gifts are significant manifestations of the common good among believers. Charisma fills the believer with prudent stewardship as his/her apply and/or dispense his/her gifts where the Holy Spirit chooses. Not all spiritual gifts are intended to bear miracle status as Peter's did. Most are not distinguished as memorable outcomes beyond the obscure location of their administration and operation. However, none are ever diluted successes or classified as mundane endowments.

Spiritual gifts are not assigned in hierarchical order. Whether mainstreamed or streamlined, visible to multitudes or observed by a few, those who order their steps with the Holy Spirit and the knowledge of Jesus Christ are blessed with a preferred sacred jewel to touch others. Such human vessels are never defined and sought out as big "I" and little "u".

"Everyday acts of service are on par with the recognized, supernatural phenomena of the Spirit. Humble, everyday service is not to be despised." (6) Consider the lad whose meager lunch launched the renowned miracle of feeding the five thousand. And, do not forget his mother who unwittingly prepared that humble meal. Simon of Cyrene, an innocent bystander, was compelled to carry our Lord's Cross to Calvary. His spiritual gift of hospitality (serving others in a supportive role) was neither insignificant or too quickly dispensed.

Simon's act continues to invoke Christian theological reflection over 2000 years later.

Simon's solitary action vividly defines the cost of discipleship. On a moment's notice, he was called to bear the cross and totally disregard human personage. In this single event, which outwardly appeared to require only physical brawn, Simon witnessed Christ and accepted the Cross. He willingly embraced the call to be crucified with Christ.

Innate in all spiritual gifts is their unifying purpose within the Body of Christ. They are distributed to individuals, local congregations and special faith-based concerns and/or circumstances. Because the gifts and bearers of the gifts live and practice their call within the Body, everyone present is blessed. This includes Tabitha, Peter, the widows, orphans and the entire Joppa community, along with Irene, the Suga-Buggas, everyone associated with the Methodist Services faith-based initiative.

CHAPTER XII

SURRENDER

"Also I heard the voice of the Lord saying, Whom shall I send, and who will go for us? Then said I, Here am I; send me."

Isaiah 6:8, KJV

ALL TO JESUS I SURRENDER, LORD, I GIVE MYSELF TO THEE;
FILL ME WITH THY LOVE AND POWER, LET THY BLESSING FALL ON ME.

(SONGS OF ZION, ABINGDON PRESS, P. 67)

When the heavenly vision engaged Isaiah, cleansing his mouth with the fire of the Holy Spirit, God beckoned, "Isaiah, come and follow me. Do not feel woefully hurt anymore. You are healed of yourself. I have purified you. Believe that you are consecrated with my holiness." (Isaiah 6:8)

When renewed by pardoning mercy and rescued through sanctifying grace, Isaiah reacted with unfainting resolve, "Here am I; send me." His doubt and suspicion of self were defeated. Isaiah's old sense of "I" changed to "we", Isaiah and the Caller together on one accord. Once again, God sends forth whom God wills. God's unmerited grace affirmed Isaiah.

Isaiah's story sheds light on the normal struggle for personal identity experienced during mid to late adolescence. This struggle is similar to that of answering the call at any age. Decisions about the future remain unclear. For the adolescent, this is the time to embrace the uncertainty which accompanies sacrifice and risk-taking. The reality of new, challenging responsibilities causes identity confusion with rebellion against the values of all authority (i.e.; school, parents, church). As adolescents seek to discover and embrace their independence, their destination remains consumed with: Who am I? Where do I fit in?

Several students in my senior high school class ended an important search for personal identity. Sacrifice and risk-taking did not deter them. Their crisis was settled. The "I" identity struggle failed to sabotage their call. They made an informed decision, believing their personal identity was integral to God's call as their most important reality.

They accepted the sacred trust of "we" in the values of divine authority. My classmates discovered "I" was incompatible when entering a relationship with God. God became the ultimate freedom and independence to embrace. These called adolescents moved beyond self and the stresses associated with their normal identity crisis. "Here am I, send me" was the essence of their decisions.

Phil announced his call to ordained ministry to his local church. After being successfully affirmed by the District Committee, he was designated an inquiring candidate. Phil entered college aware that God called him to the specialized ministry of Word, Sacrament and Order.

Joe completed his trial sermon. Now, he was under "watch care", receiving vital mentoring from his pastor and elders. Like Phil, Joe completed formal theology studies and continued to welcome the approach by the invisible, inward/personal call of God. Later, they were visibly, outwardly nurtured, tested and validated by selected Christians within the Body of Christ. At the appointed time, Phil and Joe celebrated this sacred union between God and the Church in the service of ordination.

Molly accepted Christian vocation, her profession of faith. She was preparing to enter a new life and become the bride of Jesus Christ. As a Roman Catholic nun, Molly would take the vow of poverty, chastity and obedience. Christian vocation required this called disciple to leave family, friends, fortune, and a fashionable lifestyle.

At her church, Anita, with her two first cousins, could be heard on local radio every Sunday evening. God blessed her with the tremendous gift of music. She developed her craft over the years of formal study. Anita personally knew the Lord she praised through music.

Today, these faithful disciples, who dared to release themselves of the adolescent "I" identity crisis, continue to follow their original calls as adults, nearly fifty years later. Long ago, they heard God call, "Whom shall I send, and who will go for us? (Isaiah 6:8)" From within, my classmates opened the voice of their souls with an affirming "I". Surrendering was a conscientious goal for them. Obeying God was not optional, a venture to make an autonomous decision to either choose or begrudgingly reject. Imagine all of that peace for such a long time. They took God seriously and pursued their delegated journeys with daring commitments.

The call often fails to be recognized, accepted and/or absorbed because of so much attention on "I" and the identity arises. Human innate intelligence, sensory perception, language and cognitive skills often fall short of comprehending the communicated will of God. Even with consistently faithful Christian practice, it is possible to miss the mark in the quest to encode and decode the message accompanying the call. You are assured that individuals are called to "come as you are." It is appropriate to take your identity crisis with you when you respond to your call.

God does not impart the call to perfect people. It is communicated by a perfect Caller who strives to move the individual beyond "I" identification as the rule for decision-making: I fear the risk of failure. I want my life goals. I sense my unworthiness. "I", etc., etc., etc.

"I" is only a temporary stumbling block. It is feasible to anticipate moving beyond that human frailty into the "we" embrace with God. Surrender represents the primary echo in any call. Disengage the earthly chaos which so easily belittles earnest endeavors to embrace the echo and answer the call.

The message which my classmates' Surrender advises is to: Stay still! Avoid turning off God's advances. Stop withdrawing from and being overcrowded by the barrage of earthbound noises and barriers that frequently disrupt God's call. Forget about self. Concentrate on maximizing communication. The Persistent Caller wants us to accept a sacred sense of "we" in the values of teaming with divine authority.

Chapter XIII

Just Follow!

"Now as he walked by the Sea of Galilee, he saw Simon and Andrew his brother casting a net into the sea; for they were fishers. And Jesus said unto them, Come, follow me, and I will make you fishers of [people]. And immediately they left their nets and followed him. And when he had gone a little farther, he saw James the son of Zebedee, and John his brother, who also were in the ship mending their nets. And immediately he called them; and they left their father Zebedee in the ship with the hired servants, and followed him."

Mark 1:16-20, KJV

"Pray for met that I not loosen my grip on the hands of Jesus even under the guise of ministering to the poor. That is our first task: to grip the hands of Jesus with such tenacity that we are obliged to follow his lead, to seek first his kingdom.

Mother Teresa of Calcutta

AN ACT OF OBEDIENCE

Confidently, the four Fishermen baited their hooks. Their sturdy nets covered the sea. Strangely, the waters were quietly contrary. The usual abundant shoal of fish did not appear. The prospect of an abundant catch escaped them. Without warning, their nets broke. Simon, Andrew and Zebedee's sons were captives to an unrewarding, stagnant existence. And, like the empty nets, their lives were unfulfilled. Consequently, the unsuccessful expedition reduced the four victims to a humdrum venture of sub-cortical monotony. Sometimes, people must experience failure and humiliation before they will follow Jesus.

You and I are much like these fishermen. We occasionally seek sustenance in unyielding waters, using the wrong kind of bait and tackle, armed with tattered nets to seek our rewards. We depend on these empty, porous nets for life and livelihood. Sadly, these instruments of vocation become symbols of our own preferred identity, a mark of our perceived primary purpose for existence (i.e., a hammer attached to a carpenter's belt; a broom defining self as a janitor or a stethoscope wrapped around one's neck announcing, "I am qualified to take blood pressure.") Even more critically, our "nets" cause us to have a false sense of security and entitlement. They remain glued to us much like the blanket is permanently attached to Linus, the infamous Peanuts character.

Disappointed because the troubled sea produced only broken promises, who egos now fished for pride in an unfruitful mission. More devastating, the fisherman held a broken relationship with their Lord Jesus Christ. In a mission of mercy, Jesus intervened to rescue them from their stagnant lives. It only required a single synaptic millisecond act of obedience to follow. So, when Jesus commanded, "follow me", the defeated respondents understood the expectation was to do so quickly, quietly, without quarrel.

Charlotte Elliot trusted the invitation to follow Jesus Christ, though she did not understand why or feel worthy. Our Lord and Savior was aware of her low, spiritual self-esteem. Jesus called her exactly as she viewed herself, empty and unfulfilled. Charlotte felt unacceptable to answer the call to Christian discipleship. That evening during church worship, a friend told her, "You must come as you are to the love of God."

The rest is history, for it was her newfound joy which prompted Charlotte Elliot to write, "Just as I am, without one plea, but that thy blood was shed for me, and that thou bidst me to thee. O Lamb of God, I come, I come!"[1] The decision to answer the call entails moving beyond one's perception of self. When you follow Jesus, you drop those empty nets, the old baggage that keeps the hands occupied. It demands leaving past pursuits and accepting new possibilities in Jesus Christ.

At first glimpse, one would surmise John and James abandoned Zebedee, their father. However, they believed the call had relegated them to a higher, holier parental relationship, a sacred genealogy. Jesus poses the question in (Luke 3:31-35), "Who is my family?" and qualified his purpose for ministry on earth by proclaiming; "I am about my Father's business." (Luke 3:48-50). Luke distinguishes between loyalty to genetic family ties and our responsibility to God and the call.

Jesus teaches us that the decision to follow means forsaking all others and putting salvation and service first. It demands laying aside personally held investments of earthly value such as people, property and passions. Discipleship forfeits interest in formerly chosen narcissistic ventures. Sometimes, this all-or-nothing relation with Christ while rewarding, appears to be laden with risk. The call seems endemic with failure. Confusion and mystery dominate visions about a new life of faith in the call.

Perhaps this is why so many spend an inordinate amount of time and energy discerning what God wants them to do. How shall I devote my life in service? What are the best uses for my gifts and graces? Should I continue as a layperson or pursue ordained ministry? Why should I give up what I earned for this?

Charlotte Elliot and the fishermen arrived at a crossroads in their lives. When Jesus commanded, "follow me", the idea of sacrifice seemed to be a visible safety net. The would-be disciples did not fear nor doubt the immediate shift from a safe, independent, unilateral relationship that was devoid of Christ. They immediately accepted that which was considered a risky, unknown sacrifice and depended on Christ alone. No longer was there concern for what "I" must give up to follow Christ. Quite the contrary, the newly committed disciples immediately discovered all that would be acquired when the Lord was earnestly obeyed.

STRETCH TO COMPLETE SURRENDER

The following, often told story is a vivid example of sacrifice in the context of understanding discipleship: "A family experienced a devastating fire. They lose their clothing. All household possessions were destroyed. Together, God's barnyard animals agreed to share their humble gifts. Realizing the family had no clothing, the sheep gave wool. In a sincere endeavor to appease the pain of hunger, the chicken donated eggs. The cow volunteered milk. Then, in an act of committed discipleship, the pig did not hesitate and sacrificed ham and bacon for breakfast, along with chops for dinner."

The story serves to graphically illustrate the preferred action of a disciple. We are encouraged to commit ourselves beyond safe acts of mercy and kindness. Discipleship challenges us to stretch ourselves in a complete surrender to Christ.

Follow me equates with surrendering all. All has one meaning. All means all. The goal is "to give of our souls, mind, and bodies as holy, reasonable sacrifices unto God." The call requires "all" and not a generous contribution. In return, we follow the Savior, who has given "all" by sacrificing for us on Calvary.

Herein lies the problem. Folk believe sacrifice triggers a major calamity. The contention is that giving up fame, fortune and familiarity for the call to discipleship causes compromising personal ruin or inevitable destruction. Following Christ is perceived as counter-culture. Following Christ seems fatalist, being the antithesis of the American promise of life, liberty, and the pursuit of happiness. Some fear discipleship takes them out of the mainstream to a dismal journey full of enormous bumps and bruises in the road.

We act as if sacrifice is a reality attached only to answering the call. A primary component of daily life is sacrifice. A major difference is human beings would rather do so on their own terms. We sacrifice by overextending the dignity of good credit to purchase what we cannot afford. Our children are sacrificed when we separate or divorce from our spouse. We even sacrifice our body, the temple of God, with unhealthy eating, drinking or abusive habits.

Yes, my friend, we sacrifice all the time in the secular realm. This is why Jesus continues to request, "follow me." Make the sacrifice. Surrender to the Savior. Only what we do for Christ will last.

Surrendering, for me, was quite an emotional relief. Three decades had passed since I first surmised that I was being called. Initially, the idea seemed loaded with substantial risk. The thought of sacrifice caused an inner turmoil which seemed to violate me. Also, my meager understanding of discipleship was collapsing within me. After finally following Jesus, obeying created tension. Being "able" was not my forte. Carrying the Cross offered little appeal. I lacked significant desire for spiritual formation. The rewards of giving all to Christ, against staying with my chosen professions caused a vigorous tug-of-war. Careers in higher education and physical therapy appealed to me. These choices were safe and more sustaining than a vocation which significantly demanded a total investment in Jesus Christ. I had successfully cast my nets upon the waters which, in turn, handsomely rewarded me.

Later, fear became my master. In hindsight, I recall being consumed with the thought of failing. Like the other barnyard animals, I was satisfied with only giving Christ a reasonable, self-proclaimed contribution. I preferred not having faith. After all, faith would eventually change my attitude and behavior. Believing Jesus was my personal Savior, I continued to serve the Lord with less than a sacrificial commitment. I did not relish this struggle. It was not only against the call, but more significantly, also my disregard of the all-or-none expectation.

There, I sat in troubled waters. All of my dependable safety nets were now broken and porous. I needed to be rescued by a mission of mercy. One day, Jesus came and called me from my stagnant, humdrum existence. The Caller inquired, "If Jesus were to come, would you know who calls?" Immediately, sacrifice and surrendering registered as conscientious goals. Surrendering to the invitation to follow Jesus, provided me newfound peace. It is truly a peace that is beyond any pleasantness you and I can ever understand.

THE STAR OF BETHLEHEM

Over two thousand years ago, some astrologers saw a strange but recognizable star. In its brilliant silence, it called them. The radiant beam emitted an invitation which beckoned the wise men to "come and follow!" They were convinced this was the advent of the long awaited Messiah for the world.

Being Gentiles from the east, they seem to be the most unlikely to be called for this purpose. After all, they were not guided by Old Testament prophesy. The Hebrew socio-religious culture was unfamiliar to them. Still, God called them. The Holy Spirit energized their souls. The Star of Bethlehem guided these faithful sojourners in an ecumenical procession to the newborn King, bearing informed, thought-provoking gift of gold, frankensense, and myrhh.

These watchmen had prepared for this moment. Theirs was a life full of great expectation, not a stagnant, sub-cortical humdrum existence. They were committed to Wanting! Watching! and Waiting! These persons of faith refused just to sit idlely. They did not occupy their time in denial. Their energy was not wasted attempting to gather worldly, secular holdings to take on the journey. No! Everything was left behind. They boldly followed the star to Jesus.

Jesus makes it plain. "When I come and knock at your soul's door, "Just Follow!"

- Come! Follow! Even if you believe you are inappropriate.
- Follow me in obedience. Profess a new faith.
- Follow me by living and proclaiming the Gospel. Take up the Cross. You are able.
- Follow me and find a blessing by improving the lot of the least, last and the lost.
- Follow me! Give a helping hand of hope to the hungry, hurt and horrified.
- In the name of the living God, follow me, and usher in a ray of kindness to the unloved. Have compassion for the unlovely. Receive the unlovable. You need one another.
- "Just Follow!" Become fishers of women, men and children.

Chapter XIV
Shortness of Breath

This saith the Lord God unto these bones; Behold, I will cause breath to enter into you, and ye shall live.

Ezekiel 37:5, KJV

At every stage of life the breath of God revives those spiritually dead, purifies those stained by sins, refreshes those who are weary, empowers those who are weak to make God's will their own. Rejoice! The Holy Spirit comes! (1)

DISTRESSED RESPIRATION

Nebuchadnezzar's military campaign against the state of Judah resulted in a devastating domino effect. The city of Jerusalem was ruined. The conquering King ordered the Temple to be destroyed. Consequently, the 400-year dynasty of David perished. Nebuchadnezzar placed this beloved monarchy under strictly enforced Babylonian rule. As a final blow, selected Israelites were compelled to live as exiles in Babylonia.

The effects of the Exile created several paralyzing socio-cultural problems. Unity among the tribes of Israel unraveled. Attempts to trace the family lineage in specific tribes failed miserably. The Diaspora commenced. While significant numbers of exiles voluntarily remained in Assyria, many migrated to Egypt and Arabia. Yemen granted refugees safe entry.

Inter-marriage gained widespread popularity. As a result, Israel's rich religious tradition became difficult to preserve in its original form. Subsequently, integration with the dominant Babylonia culture compromised serious faithfulness to the God of Israel. Being scattered immigrants, in the vast minority, beyond Palestine, proved to be disadvantageous in a Gentile world steeped in polytheism.

Sadly, we witness the chosen people of God desperately crying to be restored to spiritual wholeness. They are spiritually dead, unable to access the breath of God. Israel suffers from a severely acute case of Shortness of Breath.

In human physiological terms, Shortness of Breath is labored, distressed respiration. It is caused by a decreased amount of ventilation in the lungs required during increased levels of physical exertion. Subsequently, the individual suffers with symptoms of faintness, profuse perspiration, oxygen insufficiency, and chest discomfort. Victims are unable to access the great abundance of "breath/wind/spirit" in the atmosphere available for their emergency needs.

For the exiled Israelites, Shortness of Breath describes increased loss of spirituality. This is a temporary inability to access the abundantly promised breath of God in and around them. This is a weary, faith-exerting, holy breath-stealing existence. Holy essence is squandered. Divine spark dissipates in the exiled victim. Instruction of the Holy Spirit is not obeyed or pursued. The Comforter is avoided. To reverse this state of breathlessness, the individual requires a large dosage of prayer, vigilant discernment, continuous meditation and divine healing. It is time to: Stop everything! Look into the exhausted soul! And, accept the abundant breath of God.

EZEKIEL PROMPTLY OBEYED

The vision of human carnage litters the battlefield full of Israelites in Babylon (Ezekiel 37:1-14). Wevers informs that this valley is "covered with dry bones, bleached in the sun, a symbol of death."(2) Breathless souls lie in open, shallow graves. Because the bones are picked so cleanly, it is clear that the exploiting predators (i.e.; Nebuchadnezzar's Babylonian cultural influence, Israel's sin/captivity) have devoured all of Israel's hope for restored life.

> The Israelites, whom the bones symbolized, thought themselves a dead people (v.11). They had been so long dead that it was hard to image any life coming back into them. Many among them might now have realized that they were not only politically and socially no longer a people, but also religiously deceased – no longer united to their God.(3)

> Ezekiel is told to prophesy to the bones and require them to listen to the word of the Lord, in response, the Lord will make breath enter them and bring them back to life, not as ghostly skeletons but as living flesh (37:5-6). Then, the bones will know God's lordship.[4]

Ezekiel promptly obeyed. The message is forthright. He conveys the fact that Israel was caught in the bondage of physical captivity, irreligiousity and lived with spiritually destitute confidence. God intervenes to make a miraculous way out of what appeared as no way. Ezekiel promises that the mercy of God afforded more than comfort and safety. God would call the lost, exiled souls into a new fellowship. The prophet assures those born in Babylon that they would be reunited to Jerusalem.

> While he is prophesying, the bones come together and are clothed in flesh and skin – but still without life, there was no breath in them. It seems as if God's word has failed, as if the bones are after all too dry even for God. But almost before the thought has been framed, it is answered by a second command to prophesy. This time he is to prophesy to the wind, which is invoked to come from afar, bringing life-giving breath to the people. Like the Creation in Genesis 2, which was a two-stage process involving first formation and then filling with the breath of life, so the re-creation of this mighty army is a two-stage process of forming and filling. This underlines the difficulty of the re-creation process and the central role of the Spirit in bringing new life to the restored people. [5]

The Genesis Creation story (Genesis 2:7) which explains God's breath-giving phenomenon was far more empowering than the physiological exchange that transports oxygen to the lungs, heart, and systems of the body via the arteries. Neither was this equivalent to the maneuver which forces oxygen involuntarily into the life-threatened victim during cardiopulmonary resuscitation (CPR). God's breath surpassed the quality of oxygen supply some are able to hold in reserve for higher physiological levels of prolonged activity.

It was not meant to be a substitute for the first involuntary inhaled breath received by a newborn infant. No! This was God greeting God's own children from the dust of the earth. This was the new life-giving breath of God, "the first filling after the initial formation." Dead, breathless souls experienced new life.

When the breath of God floods the human body, the Holy Spirit enters and immediately begins to restore life. At that moment, every human being experiences his/her own private Pentecost. Like a rushing mighty wind, the voice from heaven reaches down into the lowly stations and speaks to all human possibilities. The dye is cast. Human disposition can be revived and called simultaneously whenever God chooses.

INHALE NEW BREATH

Has the role of disciple proven to be breathtakingly exhaustive? The people set apart with abilities to reason and accept moral responsibility must call upon God for renewal. Called to be loyal servants, they chose to embrace their earthly nature at the expense of receiving the Holy Spirit's instruction and comfort. Called to be dutiful intermediaries of righteousness, the children of God forget they are covered with glory and honor. They do not grow into their crown, but apparently choose to repel further from it (Psalm 8:4-6).

Beware! This unwarranted position of prominence, power and privilege requires accountability. The first detail is to honor and glorify God in good times (i.e.; when in Jerusalem) and bad times (i.e.; when exiled in foreign places or circumstances). The second is always to accept and prudently utilize the breath of God. Last, but not least, dutifully remember "to whom much is given, much is required" (Luke 12:48). We must endeavor to inhale new breath. God calls us to own our royal status as kings and queens.

Man and woman have profited because of their preferred status. So, why must God call? It is far too simplistic to believe the worst-case scenario. People do not go out of their way to be disrespectful or ungrateful about God's presence in their life. Being placed, "a little lower than the angels," does suggest some level of imperfection. The next questions seem to be justified. If God is in control why doesn't God exert sovereign power? Why doesn't God take immediate control over humanity. Many resemble the breathless carnage of the Babylonian Exile.

Understand, God is not merely helplessly observing human demise. Our Creator is not out of divine control. An out of control Creator is not in control of the universe. God has not become a weakling permitting humanity to become self-governing. Simply put, Shortness of Breath must run its course in earthly human will before God intervenes to restore life for heavenly affairs.

Because of the gift of free will, you and I have a stake in our destiny. In part, we choose our own fate. Whether wise or foolish, responding to or rebuffing the call, we have been granted some temporary authority over our lives. The problem is, we get trapped while making the choices available to our free will. We cannot handle the dichotomous existence, one in earthly concerns, the other in what is heavenly instructed. It's like wearing the classic Sherlock Holmes hat, apparently the same appearance between the front and back visor. Confusingly, the wearer cannot determine whether he/she is "coming or going."

Why must God call? We believe we have turf to protect, incurred entitlements to preserve. Our primary goals are to invest in self, especially as distinct and distant as necessary from the instructive presence of the Holy Spirit. Concerns abound in: Who is the greatest? I am sufficient. I have arrived. My work and accomplishments self-affirm me!

Plainly stated, we are too busy gracing our own personally valued possessions. Being human consumes our energy. Valuable time is spent at an elevated spiritually fatigue level as we venture to secure fame and fortune. Like eager beavers, we seek to build homes, bank accounts or social relationships, many times, in troubled, turbulent waters. Unlike our furry cousins, we are unable to sustain work at that torrid pace. Such antics elicit Shortness of Breath.

The Comforter has no mind to withdraw from your self-imposed exile. God is not interested in getting even with you. Shortness of Breath will not permanently destroy you. It is merely God's way of getting you to pay attention to divine advances upon you. Do not waste the Holy Spirit. Israel vividly shows that if you waste the breath of God, you will lose it.

When you are not able and/or ready to "catch your holy breath", call on the Holy Spirit to:

> Breathe on me, Breath of God,
> Until my heart is pure,
> Until with thee, I will one will,
> to do and to endure. [6]

Chapter XV

A 180° Turn

"Arise, go to Ninevah, that great city, and cry against it; for their wickedness is come up before me. But Jonah rose up to flee unto Tarshish from the presence of the Lord."

Jonah 1:2-3a, KJV

"His heart runs away with his head." (In George Colman the Younger. Who Wants a Guinea? Act 1, sc.i).

Expect Future Calls

You have surrendered to divine will, answered the call and presently live out that call in faithful obedience. Do not assume a comfortable, complacent posture. This may be only the tip of the iceberg. Expect future calls. Confidently know that new mercies may await you in another mission field. Perhaps, you are called to follow again! The next call may immediately strike you as impossible or distasteful; however, it is possible that it will fulfill your life beyond your present status.

Jonah's call to Nineveh was not his first. He served as an obedient commissioned prophet, duly summoned and set apart to be the messenger of mercy to Israel. Jonah's prophecy of consolation predicted the promised restoration of the territory in the Northern Kingdom occupied by the wicked control of the Aramean Kingdom of Syria.

When God calls Jonah the second time, it is during the reign of Jeroboam II after the time of Elisa. This era closely predates the prophetic ministries of Amos and Hosea. Jonah refuses to confront Nineveh with the message of repentance as God instructs him. Instead of obeying and going northeast, Jonah disobeys and journeys west to Tarshish. In the process, the fallen prophet turns 180° away from God, a detour of approximately two thousand miles. Nineveh is a shorter five hundred mile journey. With tough love measures, God courts Jonah's rebellion. Using serious restraint, God finally gets Jonah's attention. God intended for Jonah to respond to this call. Jonah's goal to oppose the divine plan proves to be futile.

A MORE DEMANDING CALL

This is not e-mail. God did not forward a message for Jonah to avoid. God did not accept Jonah's busy telephone signal, nor did he leave a divine message and hang up hoping Jonah would acknowledge the call at a later time. Sacred calls differ from those we receive **via** telecommunication. There is no such error as a wrong number. Nuisance calls are impossible. The Caller never has to apologize or say, "I am sorry to disturb you." The truth is simple. Ready or not, here comes God with your call.

Jonah was not ready for this frightening task. The idea of a more demanding call was totally devastating. He acted the part well. His was a direct call from God, full of specificity. Jonah chose exile and punishment. A merciful God nurtured him with deliverance and welcomed Jonah's act of repentance.

Consider with me, a modern day Jonah. He/she is riding on the highway. Consumed with self, they move to the far lane where a pedestrian signals for help. The Person looks like God. Oblivious to the divine call for help in God's Kingdom, our Jonah precedes care-free without any intentions of stopping. Then, suddenly, the sacred call forcefully blocks Jonah's road. Without any control in the matter, our Jonah brings the car to a screeching halt. Both Jonah and the brakes are fuming smoke and fire. Up go all the vital signs: heart rate, blood pressure, pulse, and respiration. A mixture of anger and visible pouting persist. "My plans are ruined; my life is now on hold. God has no respect for the direction I have chosen to go. Is not one time of obedience enough?"

Abruptly, against God's will and the traffic patterns, Jonah musters a burst of defiance and makes a U-turn. His/her illegal, ill-advised detour amounts to a decision Jonah chooses, a 180° turn and into on-coming traffic. Taking him further away from God. Our safety and reasoning is compromised when we turn our back on God.

Which direction are you traveling? If the one you choose is a detour, a 180° turn away from God and your call, the journey will prove to be a disaster. Jonah is a witness.

Hold on! Wait a minute! On second thought, continue to travel as you are. Appease your pouting anger. Exercise your free will for what amounts to a minute of God's time. Chances are you will learn something of value when the scenery changes, the road gets bumpy and your free will forces you into serious separation from God. Perhaps, a life-building lesson is at the next dead end. After all, road signs express God's command (i.e.; stop, go, yield, caution). Maybe, you need to be swallowed up into the big belly of your own disobedience.

There is the cost for a 180° turn. The great heavy-weight boxing champion, Joe Louis, makes the case in his classic retort. It seems equally relevant for pugilists who attempt to escape a formidable opponent in the ring as Jonah's ill-advised caper to avoid the call. "You can run, but you can not hide." Run!, Jonah succeeded without apparent opposition. However, he failed to hide from God's diligent act of search and seizure.

RELAX OR FIGHT/FLIGHT/FRIGHT

Jonah of the biblical text reacted with an autonomic, involuntary response, full of fight/flight/fright, devoid of purposeful rational thought. He loses focus. A lack of discernment drove him to instantaneously reject God's plan for him. Such quick self-centered, knee-jerk behavior causes a shortsighted reaction to mismanage the call. Jonah's predicament reveals a triad of hope: the reality of heavenly judgment for our self-destruction; repentant prayer for our salvation and God's unchanging mercy, along with divine forgiveness for every turn.

People do not want to stop in the middle of what they are doing something, not even for God. If what they are doing appears safe, successful and self-serving, a 180° Turn seems to be justified. Folk covet the quest for autonomy from "outside interference." "After all, God", Jonah rebuts, "I went to the Northern Kingdom, did what you required, and now, you want to take it away from me."

Relax! What appears to be a formidable, herculean task is not bound for failure and disappointment. In the whirl of human defiance, often times trapped in the belly of willful separation from God, sometimes for decades, the call continues to defy our self-determination to surrender. Someone once said, in the course of stabilizing our human affairs, it takes years of pressure to make a diamond and years of irritation to make a pearl.

Chapter XVI

Nazareth

"Can there any good thing come out of Nazareth?" *John 1:46, KJV*

"Let only the positive from your background live in you." (Frederick Douglas Sr. – my Dad)

Humble Background and Experience

Hastily, Nathaniel expressed his myopic opinion about who was qualified to carry out God's plan for humanity. What a dangerously disparaging position to assume. He challenged Philip's announcement of being called by Jesus of Nazareth with sarcastic disbelief. Nathaniel's verbal slander revealed ignorance of the Messiah's authority on earth. By posing the ridiculous question, he disclosed his slanted attitude toward a group of people based on their geographic roots. "How can it be Him?" The idea of Jesus being reared in Nazareth clouded his reasoning with doubt and prejudice.

"Nathaniel could not remember any prophecy about the Messiah coming out of Nazareth, and one stumbled at the idea of Him whom Moses and the prophets had described, belonging to such a contemptible place." (1) Fredrikson registers a similar viewpoint. "The mention of Nazareth brings a skeptical response out of Nathaniel. How can the promised One come out of a little nondescript village like Nazareth? Certainly the Messiah deserved to be from better than Nazareth." (2)

It is true. Physically, Nazareth was a desolate place. The remote town seemed to be a topographic fault, occupying the southern corner of lower Galilee. A rocky basin hid it. Viewing the surrounding country was impossible because of its low terrain. Sheen describes Jesus' hometown in sociogeographic terms. "The little village was off the main roads at the foot of the mountains; nestling in a cup of hills, it was out of the reach of the merchants of Greece, the legions of Rome, and the journeys of the sophisticated." (3)

Without apology, this was God's desire for Jesus. In an inherited locus of no apparent redeeming value to some, the world's Redeemer would frame the Gospel from the lenses of His humble background and experience. Jesus becomes the critical model of who and whose God chooses to pastor and participate in Christian ministry. Nazareth gives my Seventh and Edward Streets corner, along with your place of rearing credibility as legitimate stages to prepare for the call.

Because Nazareth had minimal interaction with the mainstream folkways and mores of Israel, neighbors sneered at its presumed lack of culture. Irreligiosity was rampant. Lax morality prevailed. Nazareth did not have a lock on such a scandalous life style. Oddly enough, this was the nature of conduct throughout Israel. This was an example of a pot calling the kettle black. Foremost, an unacceptable, dialect was spoken in Nazareth. Well-bred Judeans despised Galilean speech. It was this speech which identified Peter's geographic origin when, three times, he denied relationship with Jesus, as our Lord had predicted (Luke 22:55-61).

Nazareth did not become a respected household word of geographic or socio-religious significance until the first century Christian world gave it reverence. Mary and Joseph settled in Nazareth after returning from safe haven in Egypt. Here, Jesus was reared in obscurity. For approximately thirty years, Jesus resided quietly in Nazareth. He left home to commence public ministry at the wedding feast in Cana.

Something good did come out of Nazareth. The prophet Isaiah foretold that a "branch", would grow out of the roots of the country. This prophecy seemed to be of little value and many would subsequently despise it. "No one would ever look to Galilee, therefore, for a teacher, and yet the Light of the World was the Galilean. God chooses the foolish things of the world to confound the self-wise and proud." (4)

CALLED TO BE RESPONSIBLE

Tucked away in the booming metropolitan cities, one may find Nazareth-like pockets. New York City owns the social decay and substandard conditions of its Bowery. East Saint Louis is an infamous, inner city blight. People carefully avoid the frightening South Central section of Los Angeles. Across our nation, barrios exist full of poverty among Spanish-speaking citizens. Nazareth is revealed on the Native American reservations. The ugly head of Nazareth, like pockets, are found on farms where workers line throughout agrarian America. Appalachia, the highland region of the eastern United States, which is distinguished by poverty and lack of education, denotes the stigma of Nazareth.

Indigenous inhabitants of Nazareth are vividly reminded that Nathaniel's ghastly interrogative is alive and well. Sadly, the Nathaniel mind-set emerges when some candidates from Nazareth meet with church committees (patrons of the extrinsic call) to seek affirmation of their call to Christian ministry. What they may experience is the wrath of those called by the Church to examine and confirm their usefulness to service within the Body of Christ.

Citizens of Nazareth occasionally are not granted the full measure of the Church representative's respect. Variations of Nathaniel's question are inferred overtly or covertly. Their intention to service Christ and the Church is given marginal consideration. What seems to be paramount is gender, cultural difference and ethnicity. The opportunity to celebrate the Creator's intended diversity is abandoned. Nathaniel's question is the focus of their fear and motivation. It functions as a barrier when some committee members are called to be responsible to the Church, the will of God and the candidates from Nazareth.

A basic assumption is that the experience and background of candidates from Nazareth deviates from mainline Christian conformity. They bring mistrust which clouds any viable affirmation of their call. Therefore, citizens of Nazareth often pay a higher price for admission into the ordination process than do others. Many times they possess similar or superior local church experience, participation in denominational activities and seminary academics.

The over-arching comment in the evaluation essentially states, "rejection, nothing good can come from Nazareth." And, when affirmation is granted with lukewarm enthusiasm, the bar is raised. Burdensome contingences purposely function to stagger faith and/or drastically delay ordination.

Additionally, the guilty Christian committee members accept their call to be instruments of God. They claim to assemble to contemplate and validate candidate's suitability for ordination prayerfully. Simply put, the work of the Church is not to dissuade a fellow Christian's desire to respond obediently to God's will. The purpose is to be God's external, public voice, which confirms, celebrates, and validates God's internal, secret call to candidates. And when it is clear that the candidate is not ready to be affirmed, every opportunity should be given genuinely to assist the individual with Christ-filled support systems.

Important to this process are a culturally unbiased series of interviews, standardized testing, evaluation of written materials and a careful assessment of accredited educational preparation. Oden reminds us, "ordination committees are not made up of angels but of human beings limited in knowledge, shaped social presuppositions, and influenced by historically changing values." [5] The Nazareth question has no place among these subjective criteria.

If it is your chosen lot to be an inhabitant of Nazareth, you are an example that something good can come out of what has been deemed foreign to mainstream culture. Be reassured by the aforementioned encouragement of John Henry Cardinal Newman. "Whether I be rich or poor, despised or esteemed, God knows me and calls me by my name." You may be from Nazareth, but the ill effects of Nazareth do not have to find eternal rest in you. No one chooses his or her place of rearing. The significant point is that God chooses you. Let no one steal your holy joy. Have nothing separate you from your call. In the so-called lowest stations, God is always raising up hope and help in the midst of human error.

HUMAN JUSTICE DELAYED; NOT DENIED

At the tender age of nineteen years old, without fanfare, a promising unknown Southern Negro from a middle-class family came to Chester, Pennsylvania. He, who enjoyed a progressive culture in Atlanta, Georgia, forfeited social refinement for the working class lifestyle of Nazareth. Leaving a proud heritage, this new college graduate embraced the nagging political stench and brute selective injustice practiced in this small, industrial town. On the strength of young Martin Luther King, Jr.'s academic achievement, he could have matriculated at any seminary with more conducive surroundings. Martin chose the well-respected Crozier Theological Seminary, located in the heart of Nazareth, the infamous manufacturing hub where the eye-catching sign adjacent the Pennsylvania Railroad Station reads, "What Chester Makes, Makes Chester."

Outsiders frowned on the conservative plutocratic Republican government which employed ward leaders, along with neighborhood eyes and ears who received political patronage. Industrial company homes and government housing dotted the city. In later years, the city outlived its worldwide manufacturing reputation. Thousands fled to more advantageous locations when the Delaware River laden industry relocated across America. While Martin's unrevealed dream was much bigger than Nazareth, it's substance and focus was completely relevant to the city's lowly estimated persona. Nazareth needed the, "I Have a Dream," message desperately the day that Martin arrived. Nazareth must have been heavy on his mind when he wrote the famous speech for the March on Washington, D.C. on August 23, 1963.

Martin brought something special to this despised and rejected community. In obscurity, he quietly studied theology. Here, Martin possibly experienced a turning point which more graphically defined his original call. God graced his voice and the ability to organize the content which passed through his mouth. He was gifted with the auditory range of Luciano Pavarotti; the oratorical skills of Frederick Douglass; the poetic genius of the prophet Amos and the corresponding eloquent extemporaneous wisdom of Sojourner Truth. It was the city of Chester, this Nazareth-like locus that Martin Luther King, Jr. perfected his homiletic acumen.

Like the speech of Galieans, Southern Negro dialect and speech patterns were considered uncultured. Martin's voice transcended this common stereotype. While authentically wrapped in a Georgia accent, his articulate speech gained worldwide appeal. His charismatic phrasings cradled your ears. Martin's message was intellectually uplifting and theologically sound, while simplistic with a genius grasp of the English language.

The Southern hospitality at the Barbour parsonage helped to subdue the unpicturesque oppression of Nazareth. Here, Dr. J. Pius Barbour, Martin's father's classmate at Morehouse College, was his supervising pastor at Calvary Baptist Church. (6) Here, in the West End of the city, the would-be prophet of the twentieth century was mentored and tutored for his "holy, catholic" ministry, to secure civil rights and justice for all. Dr. Barbour was a member of the special cadre called by God to be the external, public voice, which confirmed, celebrated and validated God's internal, secret call to Martin Luther King, Jr. Just think, the Nathaniels of the time may have questioned of Dr. King, “Can there any good thing come out of Nazareth?” Thank God, he was beyond such reproach.

Citizens of Nazareth must accept being highly visible. Early in life, they learn to play on unlevel playing fields. Unfortunately, scores from Nazareth have had their call abruptly compromised by narrow-minded church committees because of their highly profiled visibility. Thanks be to God, many have discredited the myopic question posed by their colleagues called to be stewards of the extrinsic call.

Thanks be to God, there remains the vast majority on these committees, who represent the faithful souls dedicated to human justice. These Christians have not clouded their attention with Nathaniel’s spiteful interrogative. Having Christ-centered characters, they dismissed stereotypes and focused on each candidate’s call. Boldly, with great confidence they testify through their actions “something good has always come from Nazareth”.

Chapter XVII

Summoned to Simon's House

And as he entered into a certain village, there met him ten men that were lepers, which stood afar off: And they lifted up their voices, and said, Jesus, Master, have mercy on us. ***Luke 17:12,13, KJV***

> Sometimes I am in a darkness so deep, so threatening, that it seems I have been stripped of all human form and damned to an eternal solitude. At other times, I am bathed in a luminous calm, totally at peace, yet harmoniously active, like an instrument in the hands of a great master...I cannot read the score; I have no urge to interpret it, only a serene confidence that the dream of the composer is realized in me at every moment. (In Morris West's The Clowns of God, Jean Marie Barette).

IGNORANCE AND PREJUDICE

Misery dominated the daily existence of these ten lepers. Skin lesions (i.e: ringworms, psoriasis, vitiligio, leucoderma) covered their bodies. Society shunned them because the disease was presumed contagious. Subsequently, lepers were isolated from mainstream life style. Leprosy was believed to be God's retribution toward sinful people. Jewish law mandated they dress in long tattered clothing. It was expected behavior to cover one's mouth, warning approaching citizens with the degrading chant, "unclean, unclean" (Leviticus 13:45-46).

Family and close friends were forbidden to seek intimate contact with their shunned loved ones. Strict legalism caused the leper's unapologetic oppression. Congregational life in the synagogue was prohibited. Segregation requirements made it impossible to particpate in sacred Jewish community events. Ignorance and prejudice resulted in lack of any medical care. Life for the leper was spiritually and emotionally draining.

> A sense of our spiritual leprosy should make us very humble in all our approaches to Christ. Who are we that we should draw near to him that is infinitely pure? Their request was unanimous, and very importunate (Luke17: 13): They lifted up their voices and cried, Jesus, Master, have mercy on us. Those that expect help from Christ must take him for their Master. If he be Master, he will be Jesus, a Savior. They ask not in particular to be cured of their leprosy, but, have mercy on us; and it is enough to refer ourselves to the compassion of Christ, for they fail not.(1)

As the ten lepers were instructed by Jesus, they proceeded to show themselves to the priest. However, healing certification by the priest did not occur. Miraculously, the skin legions disappeared. Medicine was not administered. Cleansing occurred in the Person of Jesus Christ who never physically touched the ten. Ultimately, mercy cured the lepers because they obeyed.

Luke's gospel illustrates the perfect humanity of Jesus Christ. Luke was a physician before receiving the call to record the Gospel. With the warmth of a devoted medical doctor blessed with mercifully compassionate bedside manners, Luke proclaims the Son of Man's resolve to "come to seek and save that which was lost" (Luke19:10).

Also, the physician in Luke teaches that nurturance is paramount in pastoral care for the medically challenged. Nurturance occurs when loving attention is given to our fellow neighbor in an endeavor to support their plight to obtain mercy; protect their right to dignity when suffering from unpopular misfortunes, and encourage their faith in the mist of isolation. This is nurturing drawn out of being Christ-feeling and Christ-motivated when disease has destroyed organs and systems of those deemed unacceptable by society.

To this end, some disciples are called to act as agents of liberation for those held captive to social oppression or public offense because of the stigma associated with their medical diagnosis. Nurturance as illustrated in Luke, helps victims cope with their spiritual disease and physical disease.

The Christ of Luke conveys the idea that those called to nurture the children of God must present themselves as individuals who have personally embraced the nurture of divine presence. This means you do the things (i.e.; "walk the walk; talk the talk") which reveal how you care for yourself by placing your actions in God's hand when administering hope to others.

SIMON AND AIDS

Simon accepted the Invitation to Christian Discipleship during Sunday worship based on his Christian experience with another denomination. [2] Three weeks later, he invited me to his home. It was apparent that Simon had a heavy heart. What was this all about? It seemed that significant pastoral care and perhaps serious pastoral counseling was indicated.

Visitation ministry was always a priority for me. I believed it defined a primary role of the pastoral office. During crises, the sick, infirmed, and troubled need the intimate presence of their under shepherd to provide comfort. My professional training in physical therapy, special education and developmental psychology taught me to attend to parishioners in a variety of ways.

True, God blessed my professional background along with my vocational experience. I thought that God permitted me to carry over these skills and talents into pastoral care. However, with Simon, my journey was about to discover a different spirit for nurturance. God was about to be experienced as being active in my relationship with both Him and Simon. The old order (from my professional past) was about to change and yield its place to God's intervention in a new purpose. Vocational experience alone was history. I discovered real religious experience.

With Simon, the healing ministry defined a caring support that richly conveyed the love of Jesus Christ. My doing no longer counted. Christ worked to do in and through me. I would not approach Simon as a second career pastor with old professional talents. This call effectively stripped me of the safety valves of my professional past. At last, I experienced the charisma of divine inspiration and enthusiasm. It would prove to be a humbling, self-revealing call journey.

Confidently, I traveled to Simon's house. As I knocked on his door, Jesus was knock-in at my door. Simon greeted me with joyful affection. Equally, so did his home. It was creatively decorated. Flowers and plants blended with the aroma of the piping hot tea. Classical music always caused me to relax. I savor this moment, for it was the three-dimensional snapshot of which I will always remember Simon.

For a while, which seemed like a millennium, there was an aggravating silence. A clammy perspiration beaded my forehead. Visitation ministry had never been like this, even during the most grievous situations. I felt out of control. I knew this without knowing why. This new experience with God was disarming. This call was bound to take me to the core of my human frailty. It was not about success or failure; instead, it encompassed knowing a new compassion, a far-reaching attitude of care giving. Like the Nathaniels of the world, I had major faults to reverse. My prejudice, which I thought I had resolved, would prove to be a fresh wound within me.

Simon took a long, loud inhalation and quickly released it. "I need you to be my pastor. I am gay and dying of AIDS (Acquired Immune Deficiency Syndrome)." Simon required immediate assurance that he was a loved child of God, and that the disease was not divine punishment for his actions. "Simon, AIDS is not a homosexual disease." Our near endless joint prayer included taking turns, leading and several times speaking simultaneously with similar trends of thought. I was in a different place of loving God, neighbor and myself. My dad's basic theological foundation for his children brilliantly rang in my ears.

During another moment of prolonged silence, my mind shifted to my church parishioners. How would they respond? Some local congregations retaliated with rage, virtually driving AIDS victims away from the fellowship. When Simon finally spoke, he voiced the concern of how being an AIDS victim caused alienation above and beyond the devastation of the symptoms, signs and diagnosis. Together, we envisioned how even unsuspecting people would see him as "unclean" rather than "unhealthy", "homosexual" as opposed to "homosapien". Simon replied, "My situation amounts to a short future of feeling dehumanized while awaiting certain death."

Simon never had to deal with these emotional pains at the expense of our local church. The parishioners were compassionate and supportive of him and me. Family members continued to love Simon unconditionally as they always had.

Occasionally, when I visited, Simon's friends packed his house. The first time, I was very uncomfortable because I had no strategy for being authentically Christian in this situation. I felt like the exiled Jews in Babylon being required to sing the songs of Zion. "How shall I sing the Lord's song in a strange place?" (Psalm 137:1-4) The issue was my dormant, yet deep-seated homophobia. I thought that I had resolved this restricted love of neighbor. The full disclosure of my sin broke my heart. I heard God command "Stop! you are still running away from me, Repent!, Turn to me and be saved." Mercy enabled me to change my tune and "sing" to the glory of God in this ministry to which I was purposely called.

Like the ten lepers, Simon's friends boldly stood together. They were also AIDS infected outcasts of society. The religious community openly rejected most of them. From a distance, they sought Jesus to give them hope. In unison, their message was consistent during each visit to Simon's house, "Jesus, Master, have mercy on us". What Simon and his friends requested most was God's forgiveness. Not so much to cure their Acquired Immune Deficiency Syndrome or to relieve them of their oppressive social status, Time after time, this was their major concern.

Some of Simon's friends witnessed the wrath of their families and close friends. The local church generally proved not to be a caring, sympathetic community. It largely ignored the personal agony and concurred with the social stigma associated with the disease. The popular view was to perceive AIDS as God's retribution on sinful people. Many Christians failed to resemble the Good Samaritan or the compassion of Jesus who nurtured the Samaritan woman at the well.

Simon's friends were further victimized because: (a) bureaucratic red tape and unspoken homophobic prejudice in areas of pharmaceutical research failed to expedite production of suitable medication to suppress the disease; (b) the workplace dismissed many from gainful employment because of ignorance and rush-to-judgement, thereby denying AIDS victims adequate healthcare, medical benefits, pension, and residence in current housing.

Among Christians who were called to serve the horrified, hurt, harmed, and humiliated, the response was loud. "They reap what they sow. They deserve to die in shame." Hence, many congregations openly refused to funeralize their baptized sons and daughters, children of God. Meanwhile, the Church remained noticeably silent. The Word Jesus preached about the plight of the poor in spirit and health did not seem to apply to those suffering with AIDS. These Christians were not willing to announce freedom for the captive victims of isolation. These disciples dismissed Jesus' teaching that we should hate the sin, but not the sinner.

When summoned to Simon's house, I did not do traditional pastoral care. I experienced God. Questions and expressed personal concerns often segued into stirring biblical and theological discussion centering on social principles and justice issues. I wore several hats: surrogate parent, sibling, pastor/rabbi/priest, and new friend to persons who stood together, seeking reconciliation in the midst of physical, emotional and spiritual pain. They were Roman Catholic, Protestant, Jewish, and diverse ethnically, varied socio-economic status with one commonality – shunned children of God facing a death sentence.

REACTION TO SIMON'S DEATH

The AIDS virus began to dominate. Simon loss physical endurance. His gait became unsteady. Motor and sensory functions diminished. Pastoral care emphasis shifted. On a few occasions, once each, I took him to the pharmacy, doctor's appointment and grocery shopping. His family remained faithful to Simon during these last days. Simon just wanted me to accompany him. The idea of being in public with his pastor was gratifying. Equally, I shared this joy.

His friends were absent. Simon seriously understood why! Most could not bare to envision their future demise. One gentleman explained, "When I see Simon, I fear I see myself." Another confessed, "I must save my energy so I can die with dignity. Seeing Simon causes me to fall apart."

The manifestation of Carinii Pneumonia presented a remarkable gaunt, dependent effect. As I observed the quality of his physical well being deteriorate, a quiet scream enlarged in my gut. I missed him already. For ten months, I had visited my friend and parishioner, usually bi-weekly.

The final visit to Simon's house, several days before his last hospitalization devastated me. He looked so different from the first time I met him during the Invitation to Christian Discipleship. We completed the Order of Service for his "Home-going". It reminded me of saying "goodbye" to a favorite teacher just before graduation ceremonies. Elevated in his bed, Simon spoke in a low, quivering voice. "Pastor, I have changed your life. Some people secretly hate you. Don't you know they believe you are guilty of blasphemy? You have eaten with sinners. Some folk will expect you to end up with AIDS, infected by association. Pastor, how do you feel?" Simon was adept in his sarcastic humor which always spoke the truth.

With tear-swollen eyes and a dry, pungent mouth, I replied, "Thanks, I now see Jesus through wider, clearer lenses. Early on with you, I heard Jesus ask me, "Do you want to be healed? Take up your bed of prejudicial affliction. I call you to comfort Simon. Being summoned to your house has led me closer to salvation and immediate repentance. In you, I have found a helping neighbor."

Astonishingly, God was familiar with the root of my human intolerance. Homophobia harbored within me. The Call has a way of revealing your disfigurements. Still, God unmistakably, without second thought, chose me, the narrow, unprepared vessel; I was to be the source of Simon's nurturance. Miraculously, God, whom I initially failed, never treated me as a failure when my human frailty defeated me. God called and summoned only me to Simon's house.

Simon was an important intercessor of my extrinsic (i.e.; overt, public, person-influenced) call. Together, for both similar and dissimilar reasons, like the ten lepers, we grieved for mercy. Simon lived that I might be summoned to meet Jesus anew at his house. Early in his earthly life, Simon was called to eternally live with the Lord in the New Jerusalem. I lived to reflect personally on the call and convey to you the truth that Somebody's Knock-in at Your Door. Jesus needs you, no time to hedge.

CLOSING PRAYER

Let us pray:

Is it possible we listened only once during that initial invitation when you called us into life?

Is it possible that, though we have responded to your personal call and actively followed you, listening to your voice has been restricted to only that limited chain of events when the listening ear was primed to obey?

Jesus, Lord and Savior, is it possible that when the Gospel leads us in mission and outreach, your message rapidly fades away in favor of our lingering errant impulses to take a contrary journey?

Is it possible that our will foolishly attempts to rival the many dimensions of your call. Yet, God, you still summon us to hear you with the listening ear?

Forgive us. We fight for artificial control. We want lives that are neat, orderly and not intimidated by your habit-changing surprises. A cloud of fear engulfs us. The thought of what daily living adjustments may create if we obey the call, causes overwhelming discomfort.

If possible, even now, remove the formless dark veil which covers our physical ears. We are ready to listen. Atune us to your call. Clear the ears in our soul so that we might finally discover our place as your disciples.

Speak to encourage a conscious decision to commit to vocation, ministry, and service. Invite us again to the unknown destination with you alone. Help us to listen intently until our unseen story is transformed into visible work approved by you. So be it.

The Author

Appendix A

Focus Statement: The Call is God's created light sent to shine within the human soul. It is awareness which enlivens intentions and stimulates interest in the purpose of divine fellowship.

Topic: *"Like the lamp, you must shed light among your fellows, so that when they see the good you do, they may give praise to your God in heaven (Matthew 5:16 REB)."*

"And God said, Let there be light: and there was light (Genesis 1:3, KJV)."

And as far as the eye of God could see
Darkness covered everything,
Blacker than a hundred midnights
Down in a cypress swamp.

Then God smiled,
And the light broke,
And the darkness rolled up on one side
And the light stood shining on the other,
And God said: That's good! (1)

A formless dark veil rendered all earthly matter invisible. Deep within, encompassing the watery mass, the Spirit of God (Genesis 1:2) pranced, waiting to activate comfort and guidance in every human soul. The Word reigned with God (John 1:15), primed to reveal the crucial teachings of the Gospel to the created human order. For future disposition, God clutched countless calls of every magnitude and scope. Yet unborn, defiance, and procrastination were doomed to surrender their murky veils that desperately attempted to conceal their posture next to every call.

Unrestrained and abruptly, the commanding voice of God broke through, spreading the limitless bounds of heaven and earth, "Let there be light." Kraft adds, "and immediately, with the dazzling and wondrous blaze of a thousand atomic explosions everywhere there is light. The darkness has fled away." (2) Light proved to be a saving grace. It had been dark a very long time.

Saul lived in that dark condition. An enemy of the early church, Saul systematically persecuted Christians (Acts 8:1-3). He attended to the garments of the assassins who stoned Stephen (Acts 7:58, 8:1). On the way to Damascus to commit further mayhem against Christian disciples, Saul was dramatically immobilized by the penetrating heavenly light. With fear and trembling, he reverently fell to the ground. Suddenly, the voice of Jesus Christ spoke directly, giving him instructions for the continued journey.

When Saul opened his eyes, his sight was lost. The risen Lord elected to have Saul live in darkness without light or visible sensory cues for three days. Like many who live in darkness, he longed for the light denied him. Saul was converted during his dark condition, and called into the light of God. During those sightless seventy-two hours, Paul, the new creature, was born.

Reflection:

1. List and/or recall the types of communication with God you endured while frequenting this dark condition.
2. How did your emotional affect respond to the light in your call?

3. What was your attitude? Did you dramatically or uneventfully react, retreat, respond and/or reflect when the light shined on and in you? Refer to a call story in the Bible if possible.
4. Describe your tone. Did you verbally speak, assume some associative body language? Did you mentally ponder? If so, how?
5. Have you pursued new behaviors which either embraces or estranges the light in your call? How have you responded after being lifted from the dark condition?

Appendix B

Focus Statement: Congregations gather to be sent out to serve after hearing the Word. They do so believing they are called disciples, a corporate community of faith accompanied by the Holy Spirit. A common bond is carried in a shared vision that will not become reality until the lot of people is enhanced, made productive in quality or released from ignorance of the Gospels.

Topic: *"Where there is no vision, the people perish (Proverbs 29:18, KJV)."*

Paramount for a mission statement is a vision which vigorously assumes the work of Jesus Christ. Important components should include proclamation, social & spiritual holiness, along with transformation & reconciliation. This public document of commitment identifies who and whom congregants plan to emulate when carrying out their unified call. It asserts the deepest concerns and heart-felt critique about human need.

Because this expression of hope is vision-driven, outcomes are frequently intangible. Specific modes of intervention are often reduced to only mental impressions, not well-established goals and objectives.

However, this shared vision, should shed light on a clear picture of the congregation's prayerful choices and aspirations.

The language of a mission statement usually:

- Resembles the Cross. Vertically, it reaches toward the heavenly call for consent, while horizontally reaching out and embracing earthly needs.
- Reflects the love of God, neighbor and self.
- Is grounded in a Trinitarian theology.
- Is both user-friendly and community attractive.

Reflection:

1. Does your personal call align with your congregation's mission statement; departs from it; compatible enough for you to serve both effectively?
2. Does your congregation's mission statement truly reflect current needs/interests and today's general societal trends?
3. Does your mission statement express expectations of joy, hope, faith or is it rooted in tragedy, pain and confrontation? Why and how do you believe God is calling your congregation in your present mission statement?
4. Describe the degree to which your local church believes God's call is risk-taking. Will your mission statement have a vision to promote community economic development, evangelism, healthful/healthy living and socio-political change? Is it uniform or multi-dimensional (i.e.; serving the needs of diverse people)?

Appendix C

Focus Statement: God employs people to assist in revealing the call to unsuspecting chosen persons. They act as intercessors who are strategically incorporated to act on an individual's behalf.

Topic: *"I am reminded of the sincerity of your faith, a faith which was alive in Lois, your grandmother and Eunice, your mother before you, and which, I am confident, now lives in you. That is why I remind you to stir into the flame, the gift from God which is yours through the laying on of my hands (II Timothy 1:5,6)." REB*

The heartbeat of Samuel's call (I Samuel 3:1-21) pulsates through the veins of a mother's prayer-filled song (I Samual 2:1-10). God's tri-fold, "Samuel, Samuel, Samuel" was, in part, the culmination of Hannah's years of incessant prayer which begins during a yearly family pilgrimage to Shiloh. This anorexic woman who was unable to conceive vowed to dedicate her son to the care of Eli when he was weaned. Hannah's petition was granted. A thankful mother praised God for calling her son, Samuel, into life.

Hannah resided close by in spirit, though far away in miles while her son struggled with hearing his name. A mother's prayers unknowingly comforted her confused son. Hannah's prayers also touched Eli's soul as he intervened to prepare the lad for his call.

God did not satisfy only Hannah's intercessions for a son. Israel's religious and governmental needs were also met. Hannah's commitment to God in sacred communication provided Israel with Samuel's leadership embodied in the tri-fold functions of prophet, priest and judge. Samuel would be the last human being to hold such extensive authority until the Messiah, Jesus Christ, commenced his public ministry.

Similar prayers continue to cover you and me. It is impossible for us to lift up vividly the great cloud of family, loved ones, and concerned people who included us in their heard and unheard prayers. We have all inherited some Hannahs.

There is an old gospel truth which rings through my ears. It is sung during devotions or prayer and praise worship in many congregations. I am positive that similar expressions of these lyrics and the musical mood exist, offering a universal thankfulness for being cared for and watched over with incessant prayer. The music laden testimony reveals how scores of errant souls are guided to hear God speak to them.

Somebody prayed for me,
They had me on their hearts,
They took the time and prayed for me,
I am so glad they prayed,
I am so glad they prayed,
I am so glad they prayed for me.

Reflection:

Return and review the description of the extrinsic call in the narratives, Calls to Puzzled Ears. Then, review the narrative, Called Into Life. Give thought to the scores of intercessors who have communicated to you, knowledge of God and the call. Revisit the Hannah's who carried your case before the throne of God when you did not, could not or would not pray for yourself.

Appendix D

Focus Statement: Obeying God's call is most difficult when you are overwhelmed with the notion of what you think is impossible. Being able to assume change in an unfamiliar identity may breed contempt. Drastic shifts in roles may cause a huge sense of loss. True, Mary questioned her appropriateness; however, she immediately rejoiced in her call, "I am the Lord's servant, may it be as you have said." Mary teaches us to quickly and obediently settle into God's will. A new faith consumed Mary. Completely, she trusted the angel Gabriel's message from God.

Topic: *"To have found God, to have experienced [God} in the intimacy of our being, to have lived even for one hour in the fire of [God's] trinity and the bliss of [God's] unity clearly makes us say: 'Now I understand. You alone are enough for me.' "*[(3)] *(Luke 1:26-38)*

1. Where did you find the faith and trust in the messenger to confront the challenge of accepting your call?
2. What about your call invoked fear, threat signals or reservation? Do you feel isolated; do you believe that the same God who calls is able to provide for you as you respond to and embark on this peculiar undertaking.
3. Think about a past situation in which you originally felt unusual. Were you surprised by the unexpected or unaccustomed to being favored by God? How did you live up to the burdens of the demand thrust upon you by the call?

Appendix E

Focus Statement: Oftentimes, the who, why them, and for what purpose about the call is peculiar. God's choice of certain people and how things evolve causes the call to be described as strange. Oddly, God seems to choose from the rank and file, disregarding glaring discrepancies, deficiencies in knowledge and/or skills.

Topic: *"For ye see your calling...how that many wise men [and women] after the flesh, not many mightily, not many noble, are called" But God hath chosen the foolish things of the world to confound the wise; and God hath chosen the weak things of the world to confound the things which are mighty; and base things of the world, and things which are despised, hath God chosen. (I Corinthians 1:26-28)" KJV*

David committed adultery and murder. Although Rachab was a prostitute, God placed her in a most prominent position to establish the genealogy of Jesus Christ. Before being named Paul, Saul feverishly persecuted Christians. Prior to becoming undisputed, early Church Fathers, Origen and St. Augustine endured morally unrestrained lifestyles. Ordinary people with major baggage are chosen to answer the call and participate in extra ordinary causes for Christ.

It is true, the knock pursues everyone and anybody. God thrives on calling the least expected. In some obvious or obscure plan, all are called to participate in the spiritual warfare.

Does this include exceptional persons who deviate from the so-called norm, exhibiting significant sub-average intellectual functioning, individuals with delayed, crippling development due to pre and post-natal anomalies or adventurous accidents which require treatment, training and rehabilitation to participate in mainstream society? Absolutely! Yes! Jesus knocks to call those who live with physical, mental, emotional, and sensory challenge. Scripture usually reveals that in some manner individuals are first healed and/or restored to wholeness before their calls are revealed. The Revelation 3:20 message announces that everyone is suffering and needs the Healer. By the anointing of the Holy Spirit, Jesus claims the authority of the liberating God. His mission frees those who answer the knock. It is an arousing overture to anyone who suffers from the bonds of any type of earthly oppression, those living on the fringe of their call.

Witness the liberating call to Helen Keller. Her deaf/blind status freed the gift of genius she possessed to develop an elaborate curriculum to conquer the isolating silence and darkness experienced worldwide by human beings just like herself.

Recall Christopher Reeves. On the theatre screen, he was known as Superman. The skilled equestrian had a severe spinal injury which left him quadriplegic, the victim of total dependent care. Reeves, with an intact mind and will, and having the support of his faithful wife, answered the call to philanthropy. They donated their time, talent, testimony, and vast amounts of monies to start a foundation dedicated to research avenues to free the captive spinal cord injury victims permanently disability.

Mary Magdeline was neither a follower of the Way of Jesus Christ nor a participant in the spiritual warfare against the Way. Her own private war made her a captive. It isolated her from the knowledge of the Lord and cheated Mary of the blessing which is promised when the Lord Jesus is invited to sup with one in fellowship. Unbelievable to some, Jesus insisted on calling Mary. It was a befriending knock to call a highly visible, imperfect person. This particular call was to an emotionally disturbed, mentally challenged soul, apparently punished to fight the ghastly war against an irrational inner demonic intruder.

From within, she heard Jesus knock in the mist of her unfulfilled, troubled existence. Gradually, Mary embraced the call. She was unaware of the chartered course it would take her life. Jesus entered that isolated existence with an abundance of spiritual food.

Mercifully, Jesus healed Mary of her horrendous existence. The lessons accepted while experiencing Jesus' Galilean ministry inspired her. No longer was Mary a victim. She claimed victory in the spiritual warfare against the earthly and personal inner forces which opposed the Way, the Truth and the Light. Jesus needed Mary. Jesus called Mary to an extraordinary mission that would mend broken lives injured because of the spiritual warfare in the Kingdom of God. Freely, Mary offered her goods and valuables to support Jesus' public ministry (Luke 8:1-3).

She who lacks appropriate social skills led a fellowship of female believers to join the Galilean ministry (Matthew 27:55, 56). Mary Magdaline, who suffered years of mental arrest, was not swayed by the verbally pious indignation of the Pharisees in the crowds. The brutal tactics of the Roman soldiers failed to unnerve her while sitting at the Cross of Jesus during His crucifixion (John 19:25). Upon our Lord's death, Mary responded to the knock again. She was summoned to remain at the Cross until Joseph of Arimathaea and Nicodemus claimed our Lord's body for burial (Matthew 27:56-61). This woman who commonly envisioned distorted images was chosen to be the first human being to see and converse with the risen Lord (John 20:11-18).

Reflection:

1. Discuss the original portraits, circumstances, and the subsequent Christ-centered lives of persons you personally know, famous individuals and biblical characters.

2. Take time to discern your reality, "I may not be where God wants me today, but I am not where I used to be."
3. How does Mary Magdeline's life closely resonate with the lives of so many, including your own in the journey to leave self and receive the call.

NOTES

INTRODUCTION

[1]Scott Campbell, "Conversion or Call?" **Clergy Careers** (April 1986), 17.

CHAPTER I: SOMEBODY'S KNOCK-IN AT YOUR DOOR

[1]Matthew Henry, **Commentary on the Whole Bible.** (Zondervan Publishing House: Grand Rapids, Michigan, 1961), 1974.

[2]H.A. Ironside, Litt.D., **Lectures on the Book of Revelation** (Loizeaux Brothers: Neptune, New Jersey, 1981), 77.

[3]**Op.Cit**., 77-78.

[4]M. Basil Pennington, **Called "New Thinking on Christian Vocation"**. (The Seabury Press: New York, New York, 1983), 4.

CHAPTER IV: KNOW THAT YOU ARE KNOWN

[1]Jacqueline McMakin, **Doorways to Christian Growth**. (Minneapolis, Minnesota: Winston Press, Inc., 1984), pp. 14, 15.

[2]Doulgas Rawlinson Jones, **Jeremiah, The New Century Commentary**. (Grand Rapids, Michigan: The William B. Eerdmans Publishing Company, 1992), p. 69.

[3]Terence E. Retheim, **Jeremiah**. (Smyth and Helwys Publishing Company, 2002), pp. 49, 50.

[4]Thomas C. Oden, **Pastoral Theology**. (Philadelphia, Pennsylvania: Harper & Row Publishers, 1983), pp. 227, 228.

[5]Diana Sanchez, **The Hymns of the United Methodist Hymnal** (Nashville: Abingdon Press, 1989).

CHAPTER V: EXPERIENCE COUNTS

[1]Heschel J. Abraham, **The Prophets** (New York, New York: Harper and Row Publishers, 1962), 27.

[2]**Ibid**, 26-27.

[3]Bennie Goodwin (Editor), **Ordinary People Can Do the Extraordinary** (Chicago: Urban Ministries, Inc., 1993), 35.

[4]Dow Kirkpatrick, **Amos: Window to God** (New York, New York: Woman's Division, General Board of Global Ministry, The United Methodist Church, 1992), 6.

[5]**Op.cit**, 7.

[6]M.K.W. Heicher, **The Minister's Manual** (New York: Harper and Row Publishers, 1966), 245.

CHAPTER VI: CALLED TO VOCATION

[1]Robert F. Kohler, Editor, The Christian as Minister (Nashville, Tennessee: General Board of Higher Education and Ministry. The United Methodist Church, Third Edition, 1988), 16.

[2]F.F. Bruce, **The New International Commentary on the New Testament** (The Epistles to Colossians, Philemon, and Ephesians. William B. Eerdman, Publishing Company: Grand Rapids, Michigan, 1984), 333.

[3]Bruce, **Ibid**.

[4]Dennis M. Campbell, **Who Will Go For Us**? (Nashville, Tennessee: Abingdon Press, 1994), 16.

[5]Kohler, **Ibid**.

[6]Campbell, **Ibid.**

[7]Charles L. Wallis, Editor, **Speaker's Illustrations for Special Days** (Grand Rapids, Michigan: Baker Book House. "Ministry of Work", #713, Elton Trueblood in **Your Other Vocation,** Harper & Brothers, 1956), 165.

[8]Richard Niebuhr, **The Purpose of the Church and Its Ministry** (New York, New York: Harper & Row, Inc., 1956), 63-64.

CHAPTER VII: CALLED BY THE GREATEST LOVE

[1]Excerpts from: Frederick Douglas, Jr. **God Is Love, A Theological Perspective,** The Theology of Church and Ministry Paper, In partial fulfillment of the requirements for the degree Master of Divinity, in the School of Theology, Drew University, Madison, New Jersey, Spring 1990.

[2]Reuben P. Job and Norman Shawchuck, **A Guide to Prayer for Ministers and Other Servants** (Nashville: The Upper Room, 1983), 33.

[3]Dennis and Matthew Linn, **Healing the Eight Stages of Life** (New York, New York: Paulist Press, 1988).

[4]From documentation concerning difficulty in trusting God when sacred bonds with favored parents has been traumatically scarred (i.e., death, divorce, or alcoholism). Refer to Martin Lang, **Acquiring our Image of God** (Mahwah, N.J.: Paulist Press, 1983); William G. Justice and Warren Lambert, "A Comparative Study of the Language People Use To Describe the Personalities of God and Their Earthly Parents." **The Journal of Pastoral Care,** 40:2 (June 1986); Ana-Maria Rizzuto, **The Birth of the Living God,** a study

on formation of God-image and how it is affected by parents (Chicago: University of Chicago Press, 1979).

[5]Fulton J. Sheen, **Life of Christ** (New York, New York: McGraw-Hill Book Co., Inc., 1958).

CHAPTER VIII: CALLED TO NEW LIFE

[1]Roger L. Fredrikson, **The Communicator's Commentary,** (John). (Words Books Publisher: Waco, Texas, Vol. 4, 1985), 80.

[2]R.V.G. Tasker, Blackwell, **Bible Commentaries,** (John). (Blackwell Publishing, 2002), 67.

[3]Colin G. Kruse, **The Tywdal New Testament Commentary, (John).** (William B. Eerdmans Publishing Company: Grand Rapids, Michigan, 2003), 104-105.

[4]Mark Edwards, **Blackwell Bible Commentaries, (John).** (Blackwell Publishing, 2004), 47.

[5]Roger L. Fredrikson, **Op.Cit.**, 82.

[6]Reverend Charles A. Tindley, D.D. **Book of Sermons** (Charles A. Tindley: Philadelphia, 1932), 72-73.

[7]This is not Tindley's interpretation of his quoted sermon excerpt. The author's interpretation has been inspired by Tindley's work.

[8]Edwards, **Op.cit,** 45.

CHAPTER IX: CALLED TO UNITY

[1]William Hendriksen, **New Testament Commentary, (Ephesians).** (Baker Book House: Grand Rapids, 1967), 118.

CHAPTER X: GO! BAPTIZE! TEACH!

[1]Eastern Pennsylvania Conference, The United Methodist Church, **Annual Conference** (Journal Supplement, 1998), 18.478.

[2]Frederick Douglas, Jr., **Eastern Pennsylvania Review,** "Grace Transforms Emmanuel UMC's Parsonage." Volume 15. Number 22. October 16, 1998.

CHAPTER XI: SPIRITUAL GIFTS FOR SPIRIT-FILLED CALLS

[1]Leon Morris. I **Corithians, The Tyndale New Testament Commentaries.** (William B. Eerdmans Publishing Co.: Grand Rapids, Michigan, 2000). p.162.

[2]Leslie B. Flynn. **19 Gifts of the Spirit.** (Cook Communications Ministries: Colorado Springs, Co., 2004). p.25.

[3]Max Turner. **The Holy Spirit and Spiritual Gifts.** Hendrickson Publishers: Peabody, Ma, 1998). pp. 264-5.

[4]Gregory J. Lockwood. **I Corthians, Concordia Commentary.** (Concordia Publishing House: Saint Louis, Mo, 2000). p. 428.

[5]Flynn. **Op.cit.** p. 27.

[6]Leon Morris. **Op.cit.** p.166

CHAPTER XIII: JUST FOLLOW!

[1]**United Methodist Hymnal** (Nashville: UM Publishing House, 1989), 357.

CHAPTER XIV: SHORTNESS OF BREATH

[1]Martha E. Chamberlain and Mary B. Admas. **Hymn Devotions for All Season.** (Nashville, Tennessee: Abington Press, 1989), p. 55.

[2]John W. Wevers. **Ezekiel, The New Century Bible Commentary.** (Grand Rapids, Michigan: William B. Eerdman Publishing Company, 1982), p. 194.

[3]Douglas Stuart. **Ezekiel, The Communicator's Commentary.** (Dalls, Texas: Word Books Publishers, 1989), p. 345.

[4]Iain M. Duguid. **Ezekiel.** (Grand Rapids: Michigan: Zondervan Publishing House, 1999), p. 427.

[5]**Ibid.**

[6]**United Methodist Hymnal**. (Nashville, Tennesse: United Methodist Publishing House, 1989), p. 593.

CHAPTER XV: NAZARETH

[1]J.C. Ryle, **Expository Thoughts on the Gospel, John 1:1 through John 10.9** (Grand Rapids, Michigan: Zondevan Press), 83.

[2]Roger L. Fredrikson, **The Communicator's Commentary, John Vol. 4** (Waco, Texas: Word Books Publishers, 1985), 62.

[3]Fulton J. Sheen, **Life of Christ** (New York, New York: McGraw-Hill Book Co., Inc., 1958), 36-37.

[4]Fulton J. Sheen, **Ibid,** 36.

[5]Thomas C. Oden, **Pastoral Theology** (Philadelphia: Harper and Row Publishers, 1983), 20.

[6]David L. Lewis, **King, A Critical Biography** (Baltimore: Penguin Books, Inc., 1971), 26.

CHAPTER XVII: SUMMONED TO SIMON'S HOUSE

[1]Matthew Henry, **Commentary on the Whole Bible** (Zondevan Publishing) House: Grand Rapids, Michigan, 1961), 1472.

[2]"Simon" is the pen name utilized by the author for the purpose of this narrative. The purpose is not to compare AIDS with leprosy. The attempt is to demonstrate how some are called to unpopular settings where the social context draws public outrage and criticism. In such situations, God's call is nonetheless authentic. This reminds the reader that Jesus boldly visited the home of such an outcasted and humiliated person, Simon, the Leper (Matthew 26:1). The author's vision for these narrative is also driven by visits to leper colonies in Egypt (1963) and the dominican Republic (1996) during Mission Tours

APPENDIX

[1]James Weldon Johnson, **God's Trombones.** "Creation."

[2]Charles F. Kraft, **Genesis** (Woman's Division of Christian Service, Board of Missions, The United Methodist Church: New York, New York, 1964), 32-3

[3]Carlo Carretto, **The God Who Comes.** (In, A Guide to Prayer for Ministers and Other Servants, The Upper Room: Nashville, Tennessee, 1986), 44.